ERNST STEINKELLNER

A SPLASH OF THE LOGICAL REASON
DHARMAKĪRTI'S HETUBINDU TRANSLATED

ÖSTERREICHISCHE AKADEMIE DER WISSENSCHAFTEN

PHILOSOPHISCH-HISTORISCHE KLASSE
SITZUNGSBERICHTE, 925. BAND

BEITRÄGE ZUR KULTUR- UND
GEISTESGESCHICHTE ASIENS, NR. 108

HERAUSGEGEBEN VOM INSTITUT
FÜR KULTUR- UND GEISTESGESCHICHTE ASIENS
UNTER DER LEITUNG VON BIRGIT KELLNER

Ernst Steinkellner

A SPLASH OF THE LOGICAL REASON

Dharmakīrti's Hetubindu Translated

AUSTRIAN
ACADEMY
OF SCIENCES
PRESS

Accepted by the publication committee of the Division of Humanities and Social Sciences of the Austrian Academy of Sciences by:

Published with the support of the Open Access Fonds of the Austrian Academy of Sciences

ÖAW OPEN ACCESS FONDS

This publication was subjected to an anonymous international review process. Peer review is an essential part of the Austrian Academy of Sciences Press evaluation process. Before any book can be accepted for publication, it is assessed by international specialists and ultimately must be approved by the Austrian Academy of Sciences Publication Committee.

The paper used in this publication is DIN EN ISO 9706 certified and meets the requirements for permanent archiving of written cultural property.

ISBN 978-3-7001-9228-2

Typesetting: Institut für Kultur- und Geistesgeschichte Asiens, Vienna
Print: Prime Rate, Budapest
https://epub.oeaw.ac.at/9228-2
https://verlag.oeaw.ac.at
Made in Europe

Contents

Introduction vii

Bibliography xvii

Analysis xxv

Translation 1

Personal Names 54

Introduction

The text translated here is Dharmakīrti's *Hetubindu.* The translation has been undertaken on the basis of the only known surviving Sanskrit manuscript, which is found in the Potala. An edition of this 13th-century palm-leaf manuscript was published in 2016 (STTAR 19) based on a photocopy of the manuscript held in the library of the China Tibetology Research Center (CTRC, box 112/1). The original manuscript kept at the Potala is still inaccessible to researchers.[1]

Besides a one-folio fragment of another manuscript from the Gilgit finds (7th to 8th century CE; cf. the photo in STTAR 19: xxvix), the existence of a second 13th-century manuscript is attested through its use by the scribe or corrector of the Potala manuscript. In addition to the Potala manuscript, complete except for the broken edge of the penultimate folio, two large fragments of two further and different manuscripts have recently become available. These are contained in a collective bundle of various manuscripts of works by Dharmakīrti at Drepung.[2] Like the Potala manuscript, their scripts are early Proto-Bengālī or Vihārī; they probably also date to the 13th century CE.

The Tibetan translation of the *Hetubindu* (~ 800 CE), the extant commentaries in Sanskrit and Tibetan, and the various testimonia allowed a critical edition under the conditions then at hand. They did not allow, however, the Potala manuscript to be positioned within a stemma. Moreover, it has not yet been possible to make use of the extensive Sanskrit commentary on the *Hetubinduṭīkā* of Nepalese origin,

---

1 It can be assumed that this manuscript is also among the facsimiles of manuscripts held in the Potala in the multi-volume edition "published" 2011 with, to my knowledge, only five exemplars in the PRC. First corrections of my edition were published in Steinkellner 2016. For further corrections, cf. Steinkellner 2022a.

2 On these manuscripts, cf. my description in Steinkellner 2022. These Drepung manuscripts I meanwhile put online at Academia.edu ("A Collection of Manuscript Fragments of Works by Dharmakīrti with a Postscript by Ernst Steinkellner"). The folios of the *Hetubindu* manuscripts can be easily found with the help of the overview appended in Steinkellner 2022a.

the *Hetubinduṭīkātātparyavyākhyā* by Nayabhadra, a photocopy of which is also held at the CTRC (box 179).[3] Most surprisingly, moreover, Francesco Sferra was recently able to identify a number of folios among the Hodgson manuscripts in the Royal Asiatic Society which contain text for several lacunae in the edition of the *Hetubinduṭīkā* (Sferra 2022).

The 2016 edition of the *Hetubindu* supersedes all earlier retranslations and reconstructions[4] even though it cannot claim any certainty regarding the text's relationship to a possible autograph or early product under the eyes of Dharmakīrti himself. A number of smaller and greater differences between the two long Drepung fragments as well as the materials assembled prior to the 2016 edition and the Potala manuscript can now be examined. Yet it is beyond doubt that the text established in this edition has the character and style that mark Dharmakīrti's other works: on the one hand, the full use of the possibilities within Sanskrit syntax for emphasis, ellipsis and implication, offering perfect clarity within the context, and, on the other, a predilection, occasionally even playful, for vividly discussing contesting ideas and arguments. In light of Dharmakīrti's other works in prose, this impresses me as indicative of his personal style and manner.

The structure and style of the *Hetubindu* are also remarkable in other respects. Its core consists in succinct statements of Dharmakīrti's logic to which four digressions are added: on ascertainments (*niścaya*) (§ a.); on the pervasion between the properties of existence (*sattva*) and of being a ceasing nature (*naśvarasvabhāvatva*) which includes related ideas regarding causality (§ b.); on the nature of non-perception (*anupalabdhi*) (§ c.); and a critique of Īśvarasena's theorem that a reason has six

3 A first transliteration of folios 1–45 of this manuscript was made by Anne MacDonald in April 2004; I undertook a second reading in February to March 2021. Using the Corona quarantine, I made a first transliteration of folios 46–122 from June 2020 to June 2021 and corrected it from July to November 2021. These transliterations of altogether 476 pages are kept in the library of the Institute for the Cultural and Intellectual History of Asia of the Austrian Academy of Sciences. Editing of this manuscript will eventually be undertaken at this institute.

4 By Sukhlalji Sanghavi and Muni Jinavijayaji (1949), by E. Steinkellner (1967, I), and by Pradeep P. Gokhale (1997). A Summary based on Gokhale's edition and translation was provided in Potter 2017.

characteristics (*ṣallakṣaṇo hetu*) (§ d.). Except for the first, already dealt with at the beginning of the *Pramāṇavārttika(sva)vṛtti*, the digressions are devoted to topics not yet systematically examined in Dharmakīrti's works, or in case of the last, not addressed at all. Typical is the presentation of non-perception as logical reason. In *Pramāṇavārttika* 1 with the *Vṛtti* and in *Pramāṇaviniścaya* 2 and 3, he offers broad and comprehensive analyses of non-cognition in general and in particular, as non-perception.[5] Here, in the *Hetubindu*, he defines what kind of non-perception can serve as logical reason for proving absence and the corresponding epistemic, linguistic and physical behaviour in a single sentence (HB 26,1f) and, in conclusion, summarizes its three basic kinds (HB 33,12–34,4). But he devotes several pages (HB 26,3–33,11) exclusively to his view of the nature of non-perception as such.[6] Also, quite unexpectedly, when refuting the last of Īśvarasena's characteristics, "being known" (*jñātatva*), Darmakīrti uses this occasion to explain and defend his introduction of the term "ascertained" (*niścitagrahaṇa*) into Dignāga's definition of a logical reason (§ d.311).[7]

The presentations of Dharmakīrti's logic are elaborated on in explanations of various lengths. Some of these explanations are induced by the presence of opposing theorems. When their upholders are recognizable, I introduce the presentation of their points by "opponent," even when the opponent is defending a position that can definitely be attributed to a person, such as Īśvarasena in § d. More frequent are questions that serve for no other purpose than introducing an explanation as well as

---

5 Cf. Kellner 2001: 495–497; Kellner 2003: 121–124.

6 While this view has been touched upon earlier in various places, starting with *asatāṃ cāsattvam anupalabdhiḥ* (PVSV 4, 11f), *tatrāpy ekopalabdhyā 'nupalabdhir evocyate* (PVSV 5, 15f), and particularly in PV 4.270–273 = PVin 3.45–47b (in PVin 3. 58,9–60,9) (cf. Kellner 2003: 142–145 and Watanabe 2002), in the *Hetubindu* Dharmakīrti focusses strictly on non-perception's nature. And it is here, in HB § c.1 – c.2, that Dharmakīrti elaborately explains in what way the short statement of PVSV 5,15f is to be understood.

7 As to the fourth characteristic *abādhitaviśayatva* for whose adoption by Īśvarasena I could not find in 1967 a motivation in Dignāga's works, I am most grateful to Muroya Yasutaka for referring me (letter of Feb. 14, 2021) to a possible Dignāgean background in PS 3.27 (cf. Katsura 2009: 159f) and PS 6.15.

further explanations embedded within such a section. These I introduce by "objection" or simply by "question."[8] Such objections or questions might be understood as reflecting real questions by students during oral instruction, and, thus, could have been grounded in recollections of actual teaching sessions. Since they introduce shorter or lengthier elaborations of the preceding statements, I prefer to take them as part of a specific style of "question and answers" used for further explaining or developing a topic, perhaps, but not necessarily, on the basis of live discussions. Yet as such, they may also be considered as nothing less than Dharmakīrti's emulation of the Sūtras' hallowed prototype, in which the Buddha leads his hearers to a final point through a sequence of ever new questions and answers.[9]

On the analysis

Only recently, when I began to try my hand at an English translation of the *Hetubindu*'s text in its 2016 edition, I found with much shame that the references to the text in the "Analytic Survey" of pp. 99–110 are all wrong. These references were composed based on a pre-publication version of the text and I simply forgot to change and adapt them to the version finally published. I can only express my profound apologies to the eventual users of this edition and ask them to substitute the references published by the ones already offered in Steinkellner 2016. The present analysis differs also in some places of minor importance.

On the manner of this translation

The main purpose of the present translation of Dharmakīrti's Sanskrit text is to convey the meaning intended by the author as adequately as possible in a modern language. This conveyance of the meaning will then also serve to corroborate the editorial choices made for the edition of

[8] All these indications are in parenthesis and notwithstanding a final question-mark.

[9] Cf. for example Manné 1992.

2016 with the improvements published online later[10] with the present translation.

Departing from my earlier approach to translation, I have refrained from adding words and phrases in brackets and only use parentheses for Sanskrit terms or cross-references when considered useful.[11]

Referents are supplied that are not expressly stated in the Sanskrit, as for example, the antecedents of pronouns and substantival adjectives, unstated agents of actions, some names, and ellipses in the elaborations of a topic. Long Sanskrit sentences are separated, and extensive compounds that represent justifications are split up into individual English sentences. In general, contextually implied references are provided in order to ease the text's intelligibility. Occasional footnotes indicate the reason(s) for my choice when multiple or different interpretations are found in the commentarial tradition or in modern studies. Sanskrit *iti* is represented by quotation marks or, sometimes, before lists and the like by a colon.[12] Through all these devices, I hope, the translation will not only be useful to scholars of Indian logic, but also readable for interested contemporary philosophers and scholars of the history of logic and intellectual history in general, in particular those who do not read Sanskrit.[13]

As a consequence, it is not possible to gain from the present translation direct insights into the lexical shape of the translated Sanskrit, as was possible in my previous German and English translations, which functioned chiefly in support of the text-critical constitution or

---

10 Steinkellner 2022a.

11 For well-considered observations on the possibilities of producing readable translations of philosophical Sanskrit texts into English or other modern languages, cf. McCrea and Patil 2010: 34–40; and the recent publication of Eltschinger *et al.* 2018: 5–6.

From June 3 to 5, 2018, one could follow a lively discussion on "Brackets in modern sanskrit translations" at "indology@list.indology.info." My own reasons for using parentheses and brackets are indicated in the appendix of Steinkellner 2004: 235.

12 With this facilitation of the translation, I put up with the reader's possible irritation that objections and the like are not always followed by sentences within quotation marks; this only signifies the absence of *iti* or *iti cet.*

13 The precision of Dharmakīrti's definitions and arguments will hopefully be also seen through the present translation of his words.

interpretation of the respective edition.

In case of doubt, it is still possible to refer to the notes on my earlier German translation, even if the newly available Sanskrit text differs slightly from the earlier reconstruction.[14]

The detailed structural outline of the contents below will, hopefully, provide quick access to the *Hetubindu*'s wealth of definitions, justifications, and defences. For a search of all Sanskrit words in the *Hetubindu*, the recently published *KWIC-index to Dharmakīrti's texts* is available.[15] This index already includes the last corrections and additions to the 2016 edition in Steinkellner 2022a.

---

14 To John Taber, who kindly took a first look at this translation and rightly asked *cui bono?* I owe the feeling that this attempt to excuse myself might be considered slighting of readers who know no German. This is not intended. I simply cannot provide the contextual and systematic links again that explain the ongoing movements in this text from one point to the next. If the translation, then, may be seen insufficient for understanding, what good would it be for, indeed, and for whom?

But even without these explanations, the present translation may still be useful, primarily for any student who wants to read this Sanskrit text in order to introduce him- or herself into Dharmakīrti's logical thought.

Moreover, I also think it may be of help in re-introducing this treasure from a most creative Indian past to members of the modern open-minded Indian intelligentsia who do not know Sanskrit. The astonishingly minor success in India of selling the low-priced volumes of the series "Sanskrit Texts from the Tibetan Autonomous Region," produced in Beijing-Vienna, clearly indicates that Indian learned circles, as far as they are interested in Sanskrit at all beyond mere cultural gestures, still seem to shy away from such treasures that were successfully exiled from their motherland many centuries ago. I was not alone in hoping for better acceptance in India of these ancient Buddhist texts now available again. When starting to publish the above series, I opted for printing the texts in Devanāgarī instead of Latin script following the counsel of the late Muni Jambūvijaya, who as a leading Sanskrit scholar shared like thoughts. And now I think that an English translation might find more interested readers also in India than the Devanāgarī text, which was chosen mainly on behalf of pundits who are more or less uninterested in it. After all, the *Hetubindu* is the most ancient Indian text on pure logic that has come down to us in its entirety. But while modern India prides itself in the world for its early achievements in mathematics and linguistics, logic is rarely given comparable prominence because at the height of its development the leading masters were Buddhist.

15 Ono, Takashima, Oda 2020.

Earlier translations

After my own annotated German translation,[16] Claus Oetke published German translations, with analyses and explanations, of the digression on causality (mainly from § b.122) and other selected passages.[17] English translations based on materials available before the 2016 edition are a complete translation by Pradeep P. Gokhale[18] on the basis of Arcaṭa's HBṬ, including a newly constituted text that displays numerous differences from my own of 1967, as well as on the *Hetubindu*'s text constituted by Sukhlalji Sanghavi and the Muni Jinavijayaji in Appendix 7 of their edition of the *Hetubinduṭīkā* (1949). Partial translations are offered by John D. Dunne, of HB § 3.2 and § a.1-a.2 (HB 2,11–4,3), in his 2004 volume on Dharmakīrti,[19] and, in a broadly explanatory and paraphrasing manner, by Nagin J. Shah[20] of the sections HB § b.122 to § (b.) on the basis of the text by Sanghavi and Jinavijayaji.

In conclusion a few words may be expedient on the remarkable difference in the introduction to the first and only strophe in the *Hetubindu* from the introduction to the same strophe at the beginning of Dharmakīrti's first work which has come down to us as the *Pramāṇavārttika*'s chapter on inference for oneself (*svārthānumāna*), together with its elaborative *Vṛtti*, often referred to as the *Svavṛtti*.[21]

In both introductions Dharmakīrti says that inference will be explained, and right away starts with offering a definition of the logical reason (*hetu*). This is not a surprise because the reason is seen as the basis of inference.[22] But inference itself is also a basis, yet of what it is a basis

16 Steinkellner 1967, II.

17 Oetke 1993.

18 Gokhale 1997.

19 Dunne 2004: 412–415.

20 Shah 1967: 45–59.

21 Cf. Frauwallner 1954: 144f, 148 (= 1982: 679f, 683); Ono 1997; Kellner 2004; Steinkellner 2013 I: xv (n.5); Steinkellner 2020: 756f.

22 *anumānāśrayo liṅgam avinābhāvalakṣaṇam* (PV 2.285ab).

is stated differently. In PVSV 1,8f Dharmakīrti says: "The discernment of what is useful/beneficial (*artha*) and what is harmful/ unbeneficial (*anartha*) is based on inference. Therefore he says, because there are conflicting opinions about this inference, in order to determine it: …".[23] In contrast, in HB 1,2f he says: "Because the apprehension of objects beyond the range of perception (*parokṣārtha*) is based on inference, the following is undertaken in brief exposition to explain it."[24]

Prominent in the first formulation are the words *artha* and *anartha*, whose content can only be discerned by inference. A more precise interpretation of these terms in this context is not easy,[25] but decisive is the fact that their determination is due to inference. Inference is the means for validly apprehending within the realm of concepts and, therefore, for discerning what is conceived as useful and harmful. Inference, thus, is tasked with serving individual and social life. Yet what is useful and harmful cannot derive its scope of meaning only within the practical realm of life. Therefore, the hopes and expectations that form a larger horizon, soterial or not, within which any rational life can receive orientation, also determine what is considered as useful and what as harmful. Even if the definition of the logical reason is specifically said to have the purpose of excluding erroneous conceptions of inference, this purpose remains embedded in the determinations of the useful and the harmful in their widest sense. If that sense is Buddhist, inference that conforms to Dharmakīrti's criteria becomes a decisive weapon in the fight against all the brahmanical and pseudo-brahmanical ideologies that in Dharmakīrti's

---

23 *arthānarthavivecanasyānumānāśrayatvāt tadvipratipattes tadvyavasthāpanāya āha*: … (PVSV 1,8f).

In the beginning of the *Pramāṇaviniścaya*, inference is included in right awareness (*samyagjñāna*) which of necessity presupposes all attaining and avoiding of what is beneficial (*hita*) and what is unbeneficial (*ahita*) (*hitāhitaprāptiparihārayor niyamena samyagjñānapūrvakatvād* …, PVin 1. 1,6), and, therefore, is in accord with the earlier formulation.

24 *parokṣārthapratipatter anumānāśrayatvāt saṃkṣepatas tadvyutpādanārtham idam ārabhyate:* … (HB 1,2f).

25 Above all, there are the commentaries by Śākyabuddhi and Karṇakagomin who paraphrase the terms by *hita* and *ahita* and provide extensive explanations. Cf. Steinkellner 1981: 286; Katsura 1996; Kellner 2004: 153–157.

times were becoming ever more powerful and promoting diverging conceptions of *artha* and *anartha*.[26] Thus, this introduction clearly relates his theory of inference and the logical reason to the Buddhist soterial concern.[27]

This concern may still be implied but is not equally expressed in the *Hetubindu*'s introduction. Here, inference is only said to be the basis of the apprehension of what is beyond the domain of perception (*parokṣa*). The limitation to what is *parokṣa*, imperceptible or only conceptually given, excludes objects that are radically inaccessible (*atyantaparokṣa*), that is, are neither perceptible nor provable by reasons, but only known through various scriptures (*āgama*).[28] Such objects are not at stake here.

Further, although there are many discussions of deviant opinions on details of inference and reason in the *Hetubindu*, correcting such conflicting opinions is not mentioned as the motive for its composition. Except for the inserted digressions and a supplement, the *Hetubindu* consists of nothing but an explanation of the reason's definition as presented in the strophe at the beginning.[29] Thus, the *Hetubindu* can be considered, as far as I see it, the first work in India's philosophical traditions conceived by its author as a treatise on pure, if not secularist, logic. Consequently, Dharmakīrti devoted his last work, the *Vādanyāya* ("A Code for Debates")

---

26 Cf. Steinkellner 2013 II: 5–14 (n.4); Eltschinger 2014: 1–34 (Introduction: On Critical Examination and Apologetics) and 311–313. That Dharmakīrti's main opponents are the Mīmāṃsakas mainly represented by Kumārila Bhaṭṭa seems meanwhile to be more confirmed (cf. Taber 2021: 206–221).

27 Cf. Ratié 2017: §§ 4–11.

28 Cf. Tillemans 1986: 33–35 (= 1999b: 29–30); Tillemans 1999a.

29 Now, already Dignāga, the founder of the Buddhist logico-epistemological tradition, had composed works with the term *hetu* beginning their names: the *Hetucakraḍamaru*, the lost *Hetumukha* and, possibly, a *Hetvābhāsamukha*. But although Dignāga, in the *Hetucakraḍamaru*, surveys the formal varieties in the relationship between reason and consequent for the first time, it is still limited to this influential step in the history of Indian logic; the *Hetumukha* seems mainly to have clarified that inference is bound to the realm of conceptuality. Dignāga, then, applied his discovery to revising Buddhist dialectics in the *Nyāyamukha*, and in his last work, the *Pramāṇasamuccaya*, provided a summarizing survey of a first comprehensive epistemological system with inference dealt with in chapters two and three of six. Cf. Frauwallner 1959: 85–106 (= 1982: 761–782).

to promoting debate (*vāda*) solely as an examination of truth (*tattvacintā*) and rejected the traditional attitude of considering debate as an agonistic means for victory over opponents by whatever means.

Acknowledgments

My gratitude is due to John Taber for providing a draft translation of HB § a., as well as to Claus Oetke, who began reading an earlier version of the translation presented here and offered valuable remarks up to HB § b.113 before his untimely demise in December 2019 brought this most useful help to an end. Bertram Liyanage, the first reader of the whole translation, I thank for useful suggestions. I am grateful to Dania Huber for a first layout, to Cynthia Peck-Kubaczek for improving the English and, together with Alexandra Wedekind, for preparing the final layout, and to Patrick McAllister and Birgit Kellner for improving this introduction. My heartfelt thanks are due, moreover, to one of the two anonymous evaluators for his most helpful notes on the choice of English terms and phrases, as well as for idiomatically better presentations of some Sanskrit particles. Rarely in my life could I enjoy the pleasure of digesting remarks such as the precise ones of this reader of the present translation.

Bibliography

Eltschinger 2014 — V. Eltschinger, *Buddhist Epistemology as Apologetics. Studies on the History, Self-understanding and Dogmatic Foundations of Late Indian Buddhist Philosophy*. (BKGA 81) Wien: VÖAW.

Eltschinger *et al.* 2018 — V. Eltschinger, J. Taber, M. T. Much, I. Ratié, *Dharmakīrti's Theory of Exclusion (*apoha*). Part I. On Concealing. An Annotated Translation of* Pramāṇavārttikasvavṛtti *24,26-45,20 (*Pramāṇavārttika *1.40-91)*, (Studia Philologica Buddhica. Monograph Series XXXVI), Tokyo: The International Institute for Buddhist Studies.

Dunne 2004 — J. D. Dunne, *Foundations of Dharmakīrti's Philosophy.* Boston: Wisdom Publications.

Frauwallner 1954 — E. Frauwallner, Die Reihenfolge und Entstehung der Werke Dharmakīrtis. In: Johannes Schubert (ed.), *Asiatica. Festschrift Friedrich Weller*. Leipzig, 142–154 [Reprint in Frauwallner 1982: 677–689].

Frauwallner 1958 — E. Frauwallner, Die Erkenntnislehre des klassischen Sāṃkhya-Systems. *WZKS* 2, 84–139 [Reprint in Frauwallner 1982: 223–278]

Frauwallner 1959 — E. Frauwallner, Dignāga, sein Werk und seine Entwicklung. *WZKS* 3, 83–164 [Reprint in Frauwallner 1982: 759–841].

Frauwallner 1982 — *Erich Frauwallner, Kleine Schriften.* Gerhard Oberhammer & Ernst Steinkellner (eds). (Glasenapp-Stiftung 22) Wiesbaden: Franz Steiner Verlag.

Gokhale 1997 — P. P. Gokhale, *Hetubindu of Dharmakīrti (A Point on Probans). A Sanskrit Version Translated with Introduction and Notes*. (Bibliotheca Indo-Buddhica Series 183) Delhi: Sri Satguru Publications.

HB — Hetubindu (Dharmakīrti):

– 1. In HBṬ, Appendix: 52–72.

– 2. E. Steinkellner, *Dharmakīrti's Hetubinduḥ. Teil I. Tibetischer Text und rekonstruierter Sanskrit-Text*. Wien: Hermann Böhlaus Nachf. 1967.

– 3. In Gokhale 1997.

– 4. *Dharmakīrti's Hetubindu*. Critically edited by Ernst Steinkellner on the basis of preparatory work by Helmut Krasser† with a transliteration of the Gilgit fragment by Klaus Wille. (STTAR 19) Beijing-Vienna: CTPH–AASP 2016.

HBṬ — *Hetubinduṭīkā of Bhaṭṭa Arcaṭa with the sub-commentary entitled Āloka of Durveka Miśra*. Ed. Sukhlalji Sanghavi and Muni Shri Jinavijayaji. (GOS 113) Baroda: Oriental Institute 1949.

HBṬV — *Hetubinduṭīkātātparyavyākhyā of Nayabhadra*. Ms in the library of CTRC, box 179.

Iwata forthcoming — T. Iwata, *Dharmakīrti's Pramāṇaviniś*cayaḥ *Kapitel III (parārthānumānam). Definition der These. Übersetzung und Anmerkungen.*

Kataoka and Taber 2021 — K. Kataoka and J. Taber, *Meaning and Non-existence. Kumārila's Refutation of Dignāga's Theory of Exclusion*. Wien: AASP.

Katsura 1996 — Sh. Katsura, Karṇakagomin saku "Ryōhyōshaku dai isshō fukuchū" wayaku kenkyū (2) ["Karṇakagomin's Pramāṇavārttikavṛttiṭīkā" annotated Japanese translation (2)]. *The Hiroshima University Studies, Faculty of Letters* 56, 1996: 38–55.

Katsura 2009 — Sh. Katsura, Rediscovering Dignāga through Jinendrabuddhi. In: E. Steinkellner *et al.* (eds), *Sanskrit manuscripts in China*. Beijing: CTPH, 153–166.

Katsura forthcoming — Sh. Katsura, *na sarvathā gatiḥ*. In a Festschrift for Marek Mejor.

Kellner 2001 B. Kellner, Negation – Failure or Success? Remarks on an Allegedly Characteristic Trait of Dharmakīrti's *Anupalabdhi*-Theory. *JIPh* 29, 495–517.

Kellner 2003 B. Kellner, Integrating Negative Knowledge into *Pramāṇa* Theory: The Development of the *Dṛśyānupalabdhi* in Dharmakīrti's Early Works. *JIPh* 31, 121–159.

Kellner 2004 B. Kellner, First logic, then the Buddha? Remarks on the chapter sequence of Dharmakīrti's *Pramāṇavārttika*. *Hōrin* 11, 147–167.

Manné 1992 J. Manné, The Dīgha Nikāya Debates: Debating Practices at the Time of the Buddha. *Buddhist Studies Review* 9.2, 117–136.

McCrea and Patil 2010 L. J. McCrea and P. G. Patil, *Buddhist Philosophy of Language in India. Jñānaśrīmitra on Exclusion*, New York: Columbia University Press.

Oetke 1993 C. Oetke, *Bemerkungen zur Buddhistischen Doktrin der Momentanheit des Seienden: Dharmakīrtis Sattvānumāna*. (WSTB 29) Wien: ATBS.

Ogawa 2011 H. Ogawa, On the term *anupalabdhi*. In: H. Krasser *et al.* (eds), *Religion and Logic in Buddhist Philosophical Analysis*. (BKGA 69) Wien: VÖAW, 395–405.

Ono 1997 M. Ono, A reconsideration of the Controversy About the Order of the Chapters of the *Pramāṇavārttika*. The Argument by Indian Commentators of Dharmakīrti. In: *PIATS Graz 1995*, 701–716.

Ono, Takashima, Oda 2020 M. Ono, J. Takashima, J. Oda, *Keyword In Context Index to Dharmakīrti's Sanskrit Texts (enlarged and revised edition)*. Tokyo: Research Institute for Languages and Cultures of Asia and Africa. Tokyo University of Foreign Studies.

Potter 2017 Karl H. Potter, Dharmakīrti, Hetubindu, Summary. In: *Encyclopedia of Indian Philosophies Vol. XXI. Buddhist Philosophy from 600 to 750 A.D.* Delhi 2017: Motilal Banarsidass Publ., 475-484 with note 396.

PV 1. *Pramāṇavārttika (Dharmakīrti), chapter 1 (svārthānumāna)*: s. PVSV.

PV 2., 3., 4. *Dharmakīrti's Pramāṇavārttika with a commentary by Manorathanandin*. Ed. Rāhula Sāṇkṛtyāyana. Appendix to JBORS 24-26, 1938–1940.

PVSV Raniero Gnoli, *The Pramāṇavārttikam of Dharmakīrti. The First Chapter with the Auto-commentary.* Text and Critical Notes. (SOR 23) Roma: IsMEO 1960.

PVin 1. Pramāṇaviniścaya (Dharmakīrti), Kapitel 1: in *Dharmakīrti's Pramāṇaviniścayaḥ. Chapters 1 and 2.* Critically ed. Ernst Steinkellner. (STTAR 2) Beijing-Vienna: CTPH–AASP 2007

PVin 3. *Dharmakīrti's Pramāṇaviniścaya*, *Chapter 3*. Ed. Pascale Hugon and Toru Tomabechi. (STTAR 8) Beijing-Vienna: CTPH–AASP 2011.

Ratié 2017 I. Ratié, Scholasticism and Philosophy: on the Relationship between Reason and Revelation in India. *Théorèmes* 11/2017: 13 pp. [http://theoremes.revues.org/1966]

Sferra 2022 F. Sferra, RAS Ms Hodgson 67. Missing Pages of the *Hetubinduṭīkā* by Arcaṭa. In: R. Torella (ed.), *Italian Scholars on India. Vol. I, Classical Indology*. Delhi 2022: Motilal Banarsidass, 357–387, 433–434.

Shah 1957 N. J. Shah, *Akalaṅka's Criticism of Dharmakīrti's Philosophy.* (Lalbhai Dalpatbhai Series 11), Ahmedabad: L. D. Institute of Indology.

Steinkellner 1967 E. Steinkellner, *Dharmakīrti's Hetubinduḥ. Teil I. Tibetischer Text und rekonstruierter Sanskrit-Text; Teil II. Übersetzung und Anmerkungen.* Wien: Hermann Böhlaus Nachf.

Steinkellner 1981 E. Steinkellner, Philological remarks on Śākyamati's Pramāṇavārttikaṭīkā. In: *Studien zum Jainismus und Buddhismus. Gedenkschrift für Ludwig Alsdorf.* Wiesbaden: Franz Steiner Verlag: 283–295.

Steinkellner 2004 E. Steinkellner, The Early Dharmakīrti on the Purpose of Examples. In: Sh. Katsura, E. Steinkellner (eds), *The Role of the Example (*dṛṣṭānta*) in Classical Indian Logic.* (WSTB 58) Wien: ATBS: 235.

Steinkellner 2013 E. Steinkellner, *Dharmakīrtis frühe Logik. Annotierte Übersetzung der logischen Teile von Pramāṇavārttika 1 mit der Vṛtti. I. Introduction, Übersetzung, Analyse. II. Introduction, Anmerkungen, Anhänge etc.* (Studia Philologica Buddhica. Monograph Series 29a,b). Tokyo: The International Institute for Buddhist Studies.

Steinkellner 2016 E. Steinkellner, Corrigenda of Dharmakīrti's Hetubindu. Critically edited 2016 (STTAR 19). https://www.oeaw.ac.at/fileadmin/Institute/IKGA/PDF/digitales/Corrigenda_Hetubindu.pdf (Nov. 2016)

Steinkellner 2017 E. Steinkellner, *Early Indian Epistemology and Logic. Fragments from Jinendrabuddhi's Pramāṇasamuccayaṭīkā 1 and 2.* (Studia Philologica Buddhica. Monograph Series 35) Tokyo: The International Institute for Buddhist Studies.

Steinkellner 2020 E. Steinkellner, Dharmakīrti and Īśvarasena. In: Vincent Tournier *et al.* (eds), *Archaeologies of the Written: Indian, Tibetan, and Buddhist Studies in Honour of Cristina Scherrer-Schaub.* Napoli: Università degli Studi di Napoli "L'Orientale" *et al.* (Series Minor, 89), 753–768.

Steinkellner 2022 E. Steinkellner, Analyse einer Sammelhandschrift von Werken Dharmakīrtis. In: Vincent Eltschinger, Birgit Kellner, Ethan Mills, Isabelle Ratié (eds) *A Road Less Traveled: Felicitation Volume in Honor of John Taber*. Wien: ATBS, pp. 421–442.

Steinkellner 2022a E. Steinkellner, Dharmakīrti's Hetubindu, critically edited 2016: Further and Last Corrigenda and Addenda. https://www.oeaw.ac.at/fileadmin/Institute/IKGA/PDF/digitales/Steinkellner_2022_HB_Further_and_Last_Corrigenda.pdf (August, 2022)

Sukhlalji Sanghavi and Muni Shri Jinavijayaji 1949 — in HBṬ, Appendix 7, 52–72.

Taber 2021 — J. Taber, The Place of the *Apohavāda* Chapter in the Early Debate about *apoha*: Dignāga, Uddyotakara, Kumārila and Dharmakīrti. In: Kataoka and Taber 2021: 177–221.

Tillemans 1986 — T. J. F. Tillemans, Dharmakīrti, Āryadeva and Dharmapāla on Scriptural Authority. *Tetsugaku* (Hiroshima) 38, 31–47 [Reprint in: Tillemans 1999: 27–36].

Tillemans 1999 — T. J. F. Tillemans, *Scripture, Logic, Language. Essays on Dharmakīrti and His Tibetan Successors*. Boston: Wisdom Publications.

Tillemans 1999a — T. J. F. Tillemans, How Much of a Proof is Scripturally Based Inference (*āgamāśritānumāna*)? In: Sh. Katsura (ed.), *Dharmakīrti's Thought and Its Impact on Indian and Tibetan Philosophy*. (BKGA 32) Wien: VÖAW, 395–404. [Reprint with changes in: Tillemans 1999: 37–51].

Torella 2007 — R. Torella, Studies on Utpaladeva's *Īśvarapratyabhijñā-vivṛti*: Part I: *Anupalabdhi* and *Apoha* in a Śaiva Garb. In: K. Preisendanz (ed.), *Expanding and Merging Horizons. Contributions to South Asia and Cross- Cultural Studies in Commemoration of Wilhelm Halbfass*. Wien, VÖAW 2007, 473-490.

TS — *Ācārya-śrī-Śāntarakṣita-viracitaḥ Tattvasaṅgrahaḥ Śrī-Kamalaśīla-kṛta-Pañjikopetaḥ*. 2 vols. Ed. Dvāri-kādāsa Śāstrī. Vārāṇasī: Bauddha Bhārati 1968.

TSP — Tattvasaṅgrahapañjikā (Kamalaśīla): s. TS.

Watanabe 2002 — T. Watanabe, Dharmakīrti no hihinshikiron – sōhan kankei wo chūshin ni [Dharmakīrti's theory of non-cognition (*anupalabdhi*) – from the viewpoint of incompatibility (*virodha*)]. *Nanto Bukkyō* 81, 2002, (54)–(80).

Yoshimizu 2003 — Ch. Yoshimizu, Augenblicklichkeit (*kṣaṇikatva*) und Eigenwesen (*svabhāva*). Dharmakīrtis Polemik im Hetubindu. *WZKS* 47, 197–216.

Abbreviations

AASP	Austrian Academy of Sciences Press
ATBS	Arbeitskreis für tibetische und buddhistische Studien
BKGA	Beiträge zur Kultur- und Geistesgeschichte Asiens
CTRC	China Tibetology Research Center
CTPH	China Tibetology Publishing House
GOS	Gaekwad's Oriental Series
IsMEO	Istituto Italiano per il Medio ed Estremo Oriente
JIPh	Journal of Indian Philosophy
PIATS Graz 1995	*Tibetan Studies. Proceedings of the 5th Seminar of the International Association for Tibetan Studies Graz 1995*. Helmut Krasser *et al.* (eds), 2 vols, Wien: VÖAW 1997.
SOR	Serie Orientale Roma
STTAR	Sanskrit Texts from the Tibetan Autonomous Region
VÖAW	Verlag der Österreichischen Akademie der Wissenschaften
WSTB	Wiener Studien zur Tibetologie und Buddhismuskunde
WZKS	Wiener Zeitschrift für die Kunde Südasiens

Analysis

0.1	Motive and purpose	1,2-3
0.2	Programmatic strophe: Definition of the logical reason	1,4-5
0.3	Explanation	1,6-34,6
1.	Definition of "subject" (*pakṣa*)	1,6-2,4
1.1	Against Īśvarasena's objection to a metaphorical definition of the subject	1,6-2,2
1.2	The reason defined as a property of the subject is not uncommon.	2,2-4
2.	The meaning of "a member of the same"	2,5
3.	Definition of "pervasion"	2,6-5,14
3.1	The reason's qualification as property of the subject and as pervaded by a part of the same implies an ascertainment of positive concomitance and negative concomitance	2,7-10
3.2	The ascertainment of the reason as a property of the subject	2,11-14
a.	**Digression** on these ascertainments	2,15-4,8
a.1	Only the first experience is a valid cognition.	2,15
a.2	Why memory is not a valid cognition	3,1-4,4

a.21	Denial of an undesired consequence for the phases of a perception after the first phase	4,4-7
(a.1)	Summary	4,7-8
3.3	Ascertainment of positive concomitance	4,9-5,6
3.31	in the case of essential property as reason	4,9-12
3.32	in the case of effect as reason	4,13-5,4
3.33	in the case of non-perception as reason	5,5-6
3.4	Ascertainment of negative concomitance	5,7-14
3.41	In the case of essential property and effect as reasons	5,7-12
3.42	in the case of non-perception as reason	5,13-14
4.	The three types of the logical reason	5,15-34,6
4.1	Essential property (*svabhāva*) as reason	6,3-23,10
4.10	Definition of essential property as reason	6,3
4.11	Explanation of this definition	6,3-8
4.111	Conceptual difference and factual identity	6,3-4
4.112	The purpose of the attribute "that co-occurs with the mere presence of the proving property"	6,4-8
4.12	Two kinds of formulation of the reason	6,9-13
4.13	No further members are needed in a proof.	6,14-8,2
4.131	The formulation of a thesis is superfluous.	6,14-7,15
4.1311	The formulation of a thesis has no purpose.	7,6-15
4.132	The formulation of application, conclusion, and other members of a proof are superfluous.	7,16-8,2

4.14	The sequence of the statements of the subject's property and its pervasion is not compulsory.	8,3-4
4.15	The statement of a pervasion differs only in its formulation, not in fact.	8,5-15
4.151	Refusal of Īśvarasena's demand for both formulations	8,13-15
b.	**Digression:** The cognition of the pervasion between the essential properties of existence and of being a ceasing nature in the proof of the momentariness of all entities	9,1-23,10
b.1	The unsuitability of external causes of cessation	9,2-23,3
b.11	The incapability of external causes	9,3-10
b.111	An external cause of cessation does not cause the nature of an entity.	9,3-4
b.112	An external cause of cessation does not cause another nature.	9,4-7
b.113	An external cause of cessation does not cause the absence of an entity.	9,7-10
b.12	The uselessness of external causes	9,11-22,16
b.121	An entity ceases due to its own nature.	9,11-10,2
b.122	In defence of the above position: The reason for the uselessness of an external cause is not inconclusive because only the final phase of an entity is the cause of another entity. The example of seed and sprout	10,3-21,11
b.1221	Refutation of objections based on the presence of several causes in a single causal complex	10,12-23,10

b.12211	The final phases of the different causes do not produce the effect alone.	10,12-13
b.12212	The contributing causes are active even if one alone is capable.	11.1-5
b.12213	The contributing causes do not each produce different effects.	11,6-8
b.12214	Different contributing causes cause different properties in a single effect. The example of a pot	11,9-13,12
b.122141	Refutation of a Vaiśeṣika explanation: Since the shape of a pot is different from its substance clay, the effects are different.	12,5-15
(b.12214)	Continuation: the example of visual cognition	13,1-12
b.12215	The contributory function of momentary causes	14,1-21,5
b.122151	Causes come about as capable due to their causes.	14,13-15,11
b.1221511	A cause is not capable in the absence of other causes.	14,13-15,2
(b.122151)	Continuing: Capable is a complex of causes.	15,3-11
b.1221512	Refutation of the position that something is capable but produces together with other causes, not alone	15.12-17
b.122152	Refutation of theorems regarding the occurrence of capability in non-momentary causes	16,1-18,10

b.1221521	Introductory alternative: If a capable entity differs from an earlier incapable one, something new arises; if it does not differ, nothing arises.	16,1-3
b.1221522	Refutation of the position: a lasting entity is capable by nature.	16.4-17,2
b.1221523	Refutation of the position: A lasting entity is not capable on its own, but in connection with other entities.	17,3-10
b.1221524	Refutation of the position: A lasting entity is capable, but its effect depends on the presence of other causes.	17,11-18,10
(b.122152)	Conclusion: Contribution is only possible for momentary entities that do not occur separately.	18,8-10
b.122153	The contributory function with regard to continua	18,11-21,5
b.1221531	Also in case of a continuum the contributory character consists in the production of one and the same effect by many causes. Explanation of the arising of specific properties	19,12-21,5
(b.122)	Conclusion: Non-momentary causes can have no contributory function.	21,6-11
b.123	Summary of the arguments for the non-changeability of nature through external causes. Supplement: The melting of copper and other metals	21,12-22,16

b.1231 Refutation of the position: An entity is lasting and ceases through another. Cessation is not another nature, but the disappearance of the entity. 22,7-16

(b.1) Conclusion of the establishment of the unsuitability of external causes of cessation 23,1-3

b.2 Summarizing the pervasion between the properties of existence (*sattva)* and of being a ceasing nature (*naśvarasvabhāvatva*) 23,4-10

b.21 The general validity of this pervasion in the proof from existence (*sattvānumāna*) 23,6-10

4.2 Effect (*kārya*) as reason 23,11-25,15

4.20 Definition of effect as reason 23,11

4.21 This relationship is restricted to certain properties of the cause and of the effect. 23,12-24,3

4.22 The pervasion between effect and cause is established through establishing the relationship between cause and effect. 24,4-25,15

4.221 Explanation of entities arising from some things different in kind, such as water lily-roots from cow dung 24,17-25,15

4.3 Non-perception (*anupalabdhi*) as reason 26,1-34,4

4.30 Definition of non-perception as reason 26,1-2

c. **Digression:** What is non-perception? 26,3-33,11

c.1 Dharmakīrti's position 26,3-13

c.11	Definition of non-perception	26,3-13
c.111	As property of the perceiver non-perception is, with implicative negation (*paryudāsa*), a perception other than the perception of the absent entity.	26,3-5
c.112	As property of the perceived non-perception is, with implicative negation, the capacity for perception of an entity other than the absent entity.	26,5-7
c.113	The determination of otherness in this context	26,8-13
c.2	In defence of this position	27,1-33,11
c.21	Non-perception is absence as presence of something other or of another perception with implicative negation, not with simple negation.	27,1-5
c.22	The presence of what is other or of another perception does not prove the absence of something, but is the same.	27,6-33,8
c.221	The presence of what is other does not prove the absence of an entity,	28,1-32,16
c.2211	because the absence of something is not known as being different from the presence of what is other,	28,2-4
c.2212	and because there is no relation between the presence of what is other and the absence of something.	28,5-32,16
c.22121	The relation is not a relationship between object and subject (*viṣayaviṣayibhāva*) as between word and meaning.	28,9-29,13

c.221211	In a proof of the absence of something through the presence of the what is other, the consequent would not be a compound of property and property-bearer. The absent entity and the spot cannot be a compound when the spot on the ground is the other.	28,16-29,13
c.2212111	The relation is not possible on the basis of general and specific properties.	29,9-13
c.22122	Also incompatibility (*virodha*) is not the relation.	29,14-30,2
c.22123	The apprehension of the absence of something through apprehension of the presence of what is other is possible without a relation.	30,3-31,16
c.221231	Absence is not cognized through non-perception. Refutation of Kumārila's alternative to the position of HB 30,7f	30,13-31,2
c.221232	Absence of the other is not known through the perception of an entity.	31,3-7
c.221233	Defence of the theorem that the determination of the isolated entity excludes only that other entity which would be perceived if present	31,8-33,8
c.222	The perception of the other does not prove the absence of an entity, because there is no relation,	32,17-33,8
c.2221	since the absence of an entity is the case only together with the perception of the other.	32,19-33,8

c.23	Conclusion of the defence	33,9-11
4.31	There are three basic types of non-perception: of a cause, of a pervading property, and of an intrinsic nature.	33,12-34,4
4.311	The first two non-perceptions cannot be used as reasons with regard to entities beyond the range of perception. Rejection of Īśvarasena's theorem of "mere non-seeing" (*adarśanamātra*).	33,18-34,4
(4.)	Conclusion of the explanation of the three types of the logical reason	34,5-6
d.	**Supplement:** Critique of Īśvarasena's theorem of six characteristics for a logical reason	34,7-41,1
d.1	Refutation of the fourth characteristic: that its object has not been invalidated	34,9-36,15
d.11	Invalidation and invariable concomitance are incompatible.	34,9-36,8
d.111	Incompatibility cannot be avoided by referring to different property-bearers.	34,15-35,7
d.112	Incompatibility cannot be avoided by explaining non-invalidation as non-cognition of invalidation.	35,7-36,8
d.1121	Refutation of the position that the reason is incapable when an invalidation occurs.	35,18-19
d.1122	Refutation of the position that the reason is capable when invalidation is not perceived.	36,1-8

d.12	Non-invalidation of a reason is impossible in the presence of invariable concomitance. Thus, faults of a thesis (*pratijñādoṣa*) are also impossible.	36,9-15
d.2	Refutation of the fifth characteristic: that the singular of the reason is meant	36,16-38,10
d.21	This characteristic is already refuted by the refutation of the fourth.	36,16-18
d.22	Specific refutation of the fifth characteristic	36,19-38,10
d.221	First alternative: if there is factually no counter-reason	37,1-14
d.222	Second alternative: if a counter-reason has not been indicated	37,15-38,7
d.2221	Rectification of the misplaced appeal to this statement by Dignāga	37,17-38,2
d.2222	The correctness of a reason does not depend on the imagination of a counter-reason	38,4-7
d.23	Conclusion: There is no counter-reason in case of essential property or effect as reason	38,8-10
d.3	Refutation of the sixth characteristic: that it is known (*jñātatva*)	38,11-40,13
d.31	Cognition does not satisfy the conditions of a reason's characteristic.	38,11-39,15
d.311	Refutation of an objection against the use of the attribute "ascertained" (*niścita*) in the definition of a reason	38,18-39,15
d.3111	The purpose of the attribute "ascertained" and the purpose of its insertion	39,1-15

d.32	Cognition is implied in the second and third characteristic of a reason.	40,1-13
d.321	Refuting the consequence that positive concomitance and negative concomitance would also not be separate characteristics	40,4-13
(d.)	Conclusion	41,1
0.4	Colophon	41,2-3

A Splash of the Logical Reason

[Homage to the Sweet Lord!]

(0.1 Motive and purpose)

Because the apprehension of objects beyond the range of perception (*parokṣārtha*) is based on inference (*anumāna*), the following is undertaken in brief exposition to explain it.

(0.2 Programmatic strophe: Definition of the logical reason)

The reason (*hetu*) is a property of the subject (*pakṣa*) pervaded by a member (*aṃśa*) of the same. This is of only three types because the invariable concomitance (*avinābhāva*) is restricted to these.[30] **Others than these are pseudo-reasons.**

(0.3 Explanation)

(1. Definition of "subject" (*pakṣa*))

In this definition, **the subject** (*pakṣa*) is the property-bearer (*dharmin*) because the term for the compound of bearer and property is metaphorically applied to a part.

---

30 The interpretation of the compound *avinābhāvaniyama* is in accordance with HB 6,1f. For other explanations of the compound, cf. Dunne 2004: 150, note 16.

(1.1 Against Īśvarasena's objection to a metaphorical definition of the subject)

(Objection:) "There is here no metaphorical application, since this has no purpose." (Response:) No, because the metaphorical application serves to reject the property of just any property-bearer (*dharmin*) as reason. For in this way a property such as visibility is excluded. (Opponent:) "When the support of a property-bearer is also secured by the term 'property'—for a property is based on something else—, the bearer of the consequent (*sādhyadharmin*) in particular is obtained through the term 'property-bearer' due to its proximity." (Response:) No, because also the property-bearer of the example is in proximity. (Opponent:) Since the reason's occurrence in the example's property-bearer is established through the pervasion by a measure of the same, one comprehends only the bearer of the consequent through the expression 'property of the property-bearer'. (Response:) When the former is established, one may suspect its repetition to have the purpose of a restriction to it. Namely: In case of common absence (*vyatireka*) the absence of the reason in the absence of the consequent is stated although the absence of the reason in the absence of the consequent is established by the statement "occurrence only in the realm of similar instances." In the same way one might still suspect that the expression 'property of the property-bearer' has the purpose of restricting the occurrence exclusively to this, namely, the example's property-bearer, although the occurrence in the example's property-bearer is already established through the mention of pervasion by a member of the same. Thus, even if the meaning is implicitly understood, through a mere metaphorical application also a difficulty in understanding because of the equal indication is avoided.

(1.2 The reason defined as a property of the subject is not uncommon.

(Objection:) "If the reason is a property of the subject, dependent on the qualification through the latter, it will not extend to something else and therefore be uncommon (*asādhāraṇa*)." (Response:) No, because it is qualified in the form of an exclusion of non-connection (*ayogavyavaccheda*), as in "Caitra is an archer indeed," not in the form of an exclusion of connection with another (*anyayogavyavaccheda*), as in "only Pārtha is an archer."

(2. The meaning of "a member of the same")

Member of the same (*tadaṃśa*) means property of the same.

(3. Definition of "pervasion")

Pervasion (*vyāpti*) is the exclusive presence of the pervading property there, in the locus of the pervaded, or the presence of the pervaded property exclusively there, in the locus of the pervading.

(3.1 The reason's qualification as property of the subject and as pervaded by a part of the same implies an ascertainment of positive concomitance and negative concomitance)

On account of this pervasion by a property of the subject positive concomitance (*anvaya*) or negative concomitance (*vyatireka*) must be taken to be explained as respectively ascertained (*niścita*) by a means of valid cognition, as well as the property of the subject (*pakṣadharma*). Since anywhere the pervasion of a reason is not established in a reason with a consequent not present or there is no absence of the pervaded property in the absence of a property not pervading, the pervasion by a member of the same subject is ascertained through an ascertained positive or negative concomitance.

(3.2 The ascertainment of the reason as a property of the subject)

Among these ascertaining cognitions, the ascertainment (*niścaya*) of the property of the subject (*pakṣadharma*) is the establishment in the bearer of the consequent through perception or inference, such as of smoke at a location or of producedness in sound. For someone who through perception has seen a smoky location in its uncommon nature with a nature distinct from other things, a mnemonic cognition (*smārta*) of the inferential mark (*liṅga*) arises with the particularities experienced as its proper object.

(a. **Digression** on these ascertainments)

(a.1 Only the first experience is a valid cognition.)

Among these cognitions, only the initial experience that refers to something uncommon is a valid cognition.

(a.2 Why memory is not a valid cognition)

When such an object has been experienced, the memory (*smṛti*) arisen by virtue of the perception refers to an exclusion from what it is not, when it verbally conceives (*abhilap-*) the object's being uncommon—whatever it is uncommon with—as the difference from that. It is not a valid cognition because it grasps only the mental form (*ākāra*) which corresponds to an already experienced object. For, if after the first experience of the uncommon object it verbally conceives of this object as uncommon, it is not a cognition that apprehends something new, since only that which brings about a causal function (*arthakriyā*) is experienced, and, on the other hand, something (*svabhāva*) not yet experienced which brings about this causal function is not apprehended by a conception (*vikalpa*), as in case of an inference.

Indeed, any judicious person (*prekṣāvant*) eager for causal functions inquires whether a valid or an invalid cognition is at hand. But a universal (*sāmānya*) does not render any causal function at all as it can be grasped only after apprehending a particular (*svalakṣaṇa*) by means of a conceptual cognition arisen due to the efficacy of this apprehension of the particular, such as in case of the conceptual cognition "blue" when something blue has been seen. For it is only this blue particular that achieves the causal function to be brought about by such an entity. This particular, however, has already been experienced in this nature by perception. The causal function to be brought about by the blue particular is also not brought about by the object of the conception of blue which occurs after grasping that particular. Therefore even the definition "a means of valid cognition has an object that has not yet been apprehended" (cf. PV 2.5c and PVin 1. 20,1) must be supplemented by "when a particular has not yet been apprehended."

When the particular has been apprehended, however, the conception which arises due to the efficacy of this particular and corresponds to this particular is nothing but a memory, not a valid cognition, since it has that particular as object only in terms of being its effect (*kāryataḥ*). This is because the nature of something real not previously apprehended has not been apprehended by it, since the criterion that something is a valid cognition depends on something real. But this is so because the activity of those who are interested in that function relates to something capable of a causal function, since a real object is defined as something capable of a causal function. For, also on account of this conception one acts on nothing but something real by way of determining it as that (*tadadhyavasāya*), because in regard to an ensuing activity the successful function (*yogakṣema*) of a conception is the same as that of a perception.

(a.21 Denial of an undesired consequence for the phases of a perception after the first phase)

(Objection:) "Since in regard to a certain object the service is, then, also the same as that of previous phases (*kṣaṇa*) within a continuous perception, it would follow that its later phases are also no valid cognitions." (Response:) That does not follow, because the successful function of the phases is various when one has aims in mind that are to be accomplished through different phases. For, if the effect sought is common to all of them, the capacity of these later phases does not differ, as in the case of a nearby fire apprehended through several phases of smoke when the aim can be accomplished just by fire as such.

(a.1 Summary)

It is, therefore, denied that conceptions such as of a property-bearer, a property, and a logical mark that follow immediately upon a means of valid cognition, namely perception, are valid cognitions as well.

(3.3 Ascertainment of positive concomitance)

(3.31 in the case of essential property as reason)

Furthermore, the ascertainment of positive concomitance (*anvaya-niścaya*) in the case of essential property as reason (*svabhāvahetu*) is the establishment that the consequent follows the mere presence of the proving property insofar as the consequent is in substance the latter. This establishment consists in the operation of a means of valid cognition that negates the reason in the contradictory opposite of the consequent. For example, "What is existent is nothing but momentary. If something were not momentary, being real as its defining property is lost, because that would militate against causal efficacy."

(3.32 in the case of effect as reason)

In the case of effect as reason (*kāryahetu*), the ascertainment of common presence is the establishment of a relationship between effect and cause. That means: A relationship between effect and cause as the presence when this is present and the absence in its absence, the establishment of this, proven through perception and non-perception in the following way: "This non-perceived entity, which is perceptible as such, is perceived on the perception of that, but is not present when that is not present, even if the other causes for its perception are present." Because only in case of a relationship between effect and cause could it be said in this way for another entity "where there is smoke, there is necessarily fire," for presence only in the presence of fire is a smoke's character of being an effect of that fire.

(3.33 in the case of non-perception as reason)

Further, in the case of non-perception (*anupalabdhi*) as reason, the ascertainment of common presence is the establishment that a treatment of something as non-existent (*asadvyavahāra*) is in place merely when something perceptible as such is not perceived, because it has been demonstrated that there are no other causes for this treatment.

(3.4 Ascertainment of negative concomitance)

(3.41 In the case of essential property and effect as reasons)

Also, the ascertainment of negative concomitance (*vyatirekaniścaya*) of effect and essential property as reasons, given the established relationship between effect and cause, as well as between pervading and pervaded property, is the establishment of the reason's absence in the absence of the consequent through non-perceptions of the cause or of the pervading property the objects of which non-perceptions are perceptible. This holds for the case when the absence is demonstrated in regard of an indicated domain, since otherwise the absence of something imperceptible as such is nowhere established. The declaration of the reason's absence in the absence of the consequent in regard of a domain not indicated, on the other hand, is already established when the mere connection between the two properties is established. In this latter case, therefore, it is not required that for establishing the negative concomitance the non-perception has a perceptible domain.

(3.42 in the case of non-perception as reason)

The ascertainment of negative concomitance in the case of non-perception as reason is the demonstration of the absence of a non-perception on account of an existing entity that is perceptible as such.

(4. The three types of the logical reason)

This reason with the characteristics outlined above (cf. HB 1,4) **is of only three types**, that is, of only three varieties—as essential property (*svabhāva*), as effect (*kārya*), and as non-perception (*anupalabdhi*). For example: existence (*sattva*) as reason when something is to be known as impermanent, smoke as reason with regard to a location possessing fire, and non-perception of something perceptible as such with regard to its absence—, **because the invariable concomitance is restricted to** only this threefold reason. The invariable concomitance of the subject's property is the pervasion (*vyāpti*) as explained above (cf. HB 2,6). This invariable concomitance does not obtain in anything other than this threefold reason. It is therefore said to be restricted to only this.

(4.1 Essential property (svabhāva) as reason)

(4.10 Definition of essential property as reason)

Among these reasons, an essential property (*svabhāva*) is the reason for a property to be proved which co-occurs with the mere presence of the proving property.

(4.11 Explanation of this definition)

(4.111 Conceptual difference and factual identity)

In reality (*vastutaḥ*) the reason is nothing but the intrinsic nature (*svabhāva*) of the marked property (*liṅgin*), even though the two properties are different in terms of the exclusion from this or that other.

(4.112 The purpose of the attribute "that co-occurs with the mere presence of the proving property")

Since there is no deviation from common presence when a consequent has the reason's intrinsic nature, the qualification in the definition by co-occurring merely with that proving property is provided in view of the opinion of other logicians. For others, such as the Naiyāyikas, regard as essential property also a property that as being caused by other entities does not occur with the mere presence of that proving property. By means of the qualification, the author therefore asserts that such a property does not have the intrinsic nature of that proving property, and that the reason deviates with regard to this consequent, just as the property of being produced deviates with regard to cessation that has an external cause.

(4.12 Two kinds of formulation of the reason)

The proof formulation (*prayoga*) of this reason is twofold: in terms of similarity (*sādharmyeṇa*) and in terms of dissimilarity (*vai-dharmyeṇa*). For example, "What is existent, all that is momentary, such as a pot and the like; and sound is existent" as well as "In the absence of momentariness, existence is absent, such as in the case of a barren woman's son; and sound is existent." Such are the formulations in terms of similarity and dissimilarity which aim at presenting the pervasion in the modes of positive concomitance and negative concomitance by way of encompassing the consequent in all bearers of the proving property (*sarvopasaṃhāra*).

(4.13 No further members are needed in a proof.)

(4.131 The formulation of a thesis is superfluous.)

Among these two types of proof formulations, there is no formulation of a thesis (*pratijñā*) because one apprehends the subject of the thesis already by implication. (Objection:) "If what is to be apprehended is not indicated, how is it apprehended?" (Response:) If one apprehends by oneself, who would indicate what is to be apprehended? When someone perceiving smoke that hovers over a location recollects its pervasion by fire, the cognition "there is fire" unfolds already by force of these cognitions. But no one tells him at this occasion that there is fire. Nor does he know something himself already before a reason is at hand. This is because without a means of cognition, namely a reason, there is no ground for a cognition in this manner, or because otherwise a logical mark would be futile if such a cognition were around. What sequence of apprehensions would this be, when someone just on his own decided by chance something to be apprehended, namely, that there is fire, and then again in order to apprehend it looks for a logical mark? Also, when that which is to be apprehended is stated by another person, it certainly fades away since there is no use of it.

(4.1311 The formulation of a thesis has no purpose.)

(Objection:) "The application of a thesis is to indicate the reason's object, the consequent." (Response:) What, to begin with, is the advantage when precisely this has been indicated? If the intended cognition would otherwise not come about, then all this would be fine. Therefore, knowing it even without any provision of the object through someone when he knows by himself, he sees us intent on it and, then, asks for a plain fee in form of a thesis, like a Brahmin who charges for irregular rituals. Even upon a formulation provided by us he knows the object only in betaking himself to the logical mark he has already established himself. What, then, is the difference between these two situations of indicating and not indicating a thesis? But the resulting inferential cognition is known even without the formulation of a thesis on account of the mere formulations of the subject's property and its relation. What, therefore, is the use of this formulation of a thesis? But a proof (*sādhana*) is brought forward in order to induce a determinate cognition (*niścaya*) in other persons comparable to one's own determinate cognition. What is the motive for the fact that an inferring person, when in this case knowing it himself even without an indication of what is to be apprehended, when expounding it to another person relies on a new order of purpose? Therefore, a formulation of what is to be apprehended is of no use, because its apprehension comes about in another way as well.

(4.132 The formulation of application, conclusion, and other members of a proof are superfluous.)

For this reason, also other members of a proof such as application (*upanaya*) and conclusion (*nigamana*) are rejected, because the acknowledgement as a proof-statement (*vākya*) ensues through a formulation to precisely the extent mentioned above (cf. HB 6,9-13). Thus, abstain from this clownish passion, close your eyes, and consider first: Would the consequent be cognized through this amount of proof members or not? If it is, what good is in a string of prolixity? Consequently, the formulation in a proof statement to precisely the extent above explained is superior.

(4.14 The sequence of the statements of the subject's property and its pervasion is not compulsory.)

Moreover, in this formulation of a proof the sequence of the statements of the subject's property (*pakṣadharma*) and the relation (*sambandha*) is not fixed, because it is indicative in both ways.

(4.15 The statement of a pervasion differs only in its formulation, not in fact.)

Also in case of the statement of the relation (*sambandha*) only the formulation differs, not the meaning (*artha*), for in both ways, even if the properties differ, nothing is conveyed but the fact that the proving property is the intrinsic nature of the consequent. For, if a property which does not have the intrinsic nature of the other is present, that other property is not necessarily present, such as having the property of arising through an effort (*prayatnotpattidharmatā*) is not necessarily present when the property to be produced is present. Also that property is not absent if a property which does not have its intrinsic nature is absent, given it is not an effect; for example, these same two properties in reverse. Therefore, even one of the two, positive or negative concomitances as defined above (cf. HB 6,9-13), indicates as employed the second. Thus, we are not in favour of the formulation of both in a single statement of proof, because it is useless. For, when the positive concomitance of that property is established through the fact that it has the intrinsic nature of the other, the absence of the latter in the absence of the former is established, and when its absence is established in the absence of the former, their positive concomitance is established.

(4.151 Refusal of Īśvarasena's demand for both formulations)

A separate formulation of negative concomitance is also not appropriate with the purpose of communicating the restriction that the designation of absence may only be applied to the absence of the consequent, but not to what is other than what is similar or to what is in contradiction to what is similar,[31] because also what is other and what is in contradiction is something dissimilar (*vipakṣa*).

(b. **Digression:** The cognition of the pervasion between the essential properties of existence and of being a ceasing nature in the proof of the momentariness of all entities)

(Question:) How is it, now, apprehended that the intrinsic nature of an existent entity is necessarily ceasing (cf. HB 5,16), so that common presence and absence of these properties would be given in the proof of momentariness?

---

[31] The assumption of this purpose of a separate formulation of negative concomitance derives from Īśvarasena's lost commentary on PSV on PS 3.19.

(b.1 The unsuitability of external causes of cessation)

(Response:) Because external causes of cessation (*vināśahetu*) are unsuitable. Entities cease only on account of their intrinsic nature (*svabhāvataḥ*).

(b.11 The incapability of external causes)

The cessation of these accomplished entities does not come about through another entity, because that would be incapable (*asāmarthya*) of causing it.

(b.111 An external cause of cessation does not cause the nature of an entity.)

For, an external cause of cessation does not cause the very nature of an entity, because this nature has been accomplished through something else, namely already through its own causes.

(b.112 An external cause of cessation does not cause another nature.)

Moreover, if a cause of cessation caused another nature, it would mean nothing for the entity in question that remains in the same state. Thus, it would follow that the entity would still be perceived and so on. A concealing (*āvaraṇa*) of this entity in question, too, would not be another nature, because also a concealing is not suitable for this entity that remains in the same state.

(b.113 An external cause of cessation does not cause the absence of an entity.)

Nor does an external cause of cessation cause the absence of an entity. Since, if one assumes that absence is an effect by affirmation, i.e., by way of an implicative negation, there is no overcoming the alternative of difference and non-difference. But if absence is the simple negation of an entity, it would be the case that this cause does not produce an entity. But since in these ways what does not produce something is not a cause, nothing would be an external cause of cessation.

(b.12 The uselessness of external causes)

Also because external causes are useless (*vaiyarthya*).

(b.121 An entity ceases due to its own nature.)

If an entity ceases due to its nature, an external cause serves it in no way because it ceases by itself through nothing but the fact that it has that ceasing nature. For what nature something has, it is like that when it arises from nothing but its own causes. It does not again depend on other causes for being like that (cf. HB 21,12f), such as bright, fluid, hot and hard substances and so on. For, entities such as bright ones which have arisen with that nature do not further require another cause for being bright and so on, because if something of that nature were not to have that nature, it would consequently be without a nature. In the same way, if an entity has been produced in terms of its nature with the property of instability (*asthiti*), it does not further require another cause for having that nature.

(b.122 In defence of the above position: The reason for the use-lessness of an external cause is not inconclusive because only the final phase of an entity is the cause of another entity. The example of seed and sprout)

(Objection:) "The reason for the uselessness of an external cause given above (HB b.121) is inconclusive (*anekānta*), as in the case of seed and so on." That is to say: "Although seed and the like exist with the nature to produce a sprout and the like, they do not produce these in isolation since they require other causes such as water. Similarly also an entity would require other causes for its cessation."

(Response:) This inconclusiveness does not obtain because what is of that nature produces, and what does not produce is not of that nature. Precisely therefore a difference in the real entities is to be taken for granted between these two states of producing and non-producing. For, because entities do not change their nature, an entity which has that producing nature would consequently produce already earlier as it does later. Therefore only the final, specific state of a seed and so on has the nature of producing a sprout and so on. The preceding specific states in the continuum of seed phases, however, are only the causes of this final cause. The reason for the uselessness of external causes is, thus, not inconclusive, for in momentary entities there is no unity, since they arise from ever other phases.

(b.1221 Refutation of objections based on the presence of several causes in a single causal complex)

(b.12211 The final phases of the different causes do not produce the effect alone.)

(Question:) "Why do these final capable causes not each produce?" (Response:) They certainly produce. With respect to producing they do not change, because their nature is not inconsistent.

(b.12212 The contributing causes are active even if one alone is capable.)

(Question:) "If all these contributing causes are each of capable nature, what would the respective other causes serve for?" (Response:) Surely entities have no activity preceded by deliberation so that the other causes would abstain on thinking "capable is this single one even alone. What could be our task in this matter?" For these entities that operate without intentions and have the property of being near to each other through a transformation in their own causes do not deserve to be blamed for being so because of their nature.

(b.12213 The contributing causes do not each produce different effects.)

(Question:) "Why do contributing causes that are capable not produce different effects respectively?" (Response:) They do not, because as contributing causes they are capable only with regard to this, namely, this single effect. Since they are capable of producing precisely this single effect and not another, they do not each produce different effects.

(b.12214 Different contributing causes cause different properties in a single effect. The example of a pot)

(Objection:) "If through the contributing causes eyes and so on with different natures a single effect were produced, different effects would not come about through different causes." (Response:) This does not follow. Because the contributing causes, in their respectively different nature, contribute to the specific characters of the effect, and therefore the specific characters of the nature to be effected by these causes' contribution are not conflated. For example: For a pot produced through a complex of causes such as a lump of clay, a potter, and a thread, a nature comes about on account of the lump of clay which is distinct from things such as a tree that are not of the nature of clay. On account of the potter for the same pot, while it consists of clay, through having the nature of a specific shape of clay a nature comes about which is distinct from others than this clay product. On account of the thread for the same pot that is of the nature of clay and of a specific shape, a nature comes about that is different from a disc and the like. In this way, therefore, neither does the pot have the nature of clay due to the potter, nor is the specific shape due to the clay. Yet, even if the causal domain of the specific capacities of these two causes is different, the effect with its different specific characters produced by these causes does not differ in its nature. For, otherwise, due to the fact that clay and shape do not have the nature of the respective other, it would follow that these two could not appear in cognition with the specific natures of shape and clay, respectively.

(b.122141 Refutation of a Vaiśeṣika explanation: Since the shape of a pot is different from its substance clay, the effects are different.)

(Opponent:) "Shape (*saṃsthāna*) as a quality (*guṇa*) is certainly something else than the substance clay. Therefore a different nature, respectively, is the causal domain for the contribution of the potter and the lump of clay."

(Response:) This point we have already addressed (cf. HB 12,3f). Moreover, if the pot's shape were different from the clay, why does the potter not produce it separately?

(Opponent:) The shape is not brought about separately because as quality it depends on a substance. Thus, if the Buddhist asks "This substance clay which is by nature the support of that shape, or its shape which is by nature what is supported by this substance, why do they depend on a potter?" we answer: This is no objection, for they depend on a potter because their capacity to be mutually connected is attained through that potter. Otherwise, if the capacity of the lump of clay to be connected with a specific shape were given even before the potter's presence, it follows that the connection with a specific shape would already be given through the mere fact that it is a property of the stuff clay.

(Response:) In this way, then, this capacity of the substance of clay would be due to the potter. But the natures of these two, clay and its capacity, are not distinct. For, if they were distinct, the consequence would be as above (HB 12,7), namely, that the potter could produce these separately. There is, therefore, indeed a certain fact that distinctions are caused by many causes, even if something has only a single nature. Thus, we do not insist on proving that clay and its shape are of one and the same nature.

(b.12214 Continuation: the example of visual cognition)

Contributing causes, therefore, do not have a single domain for their assistance, although the effect's nature, in reality, is single. Thus, as in this case of a pot and its causes, different causes do not have a single effect because they contribute to different specific properties, so is it to be presumed when a cognition arises through eyes and other senses. That is to say: That a visual cognition has the nature of cognition is due to cognition as the immediately preceding homogeneous cause (*samanantarapratyaya*). While it is cognition by nature, the restriction of the same to a capacity for grasping visibles (*rūpa*) is due to the sense of the eyes. Due to the object is the fact that cognition has a form like this object. Thus, quite different essential properties result due to the different natures of the effect's causes, although the effect is in reality not different. Even though, therefore, the contributing causes are different, the thereby resulting essential properties are not non-different. For this reason, exactly these different capacities of the causes are engaged due to the fact that the capacities for producing the specific effects respectively cannot be impeded, and because of their momentariness are referred to as the basis for the presence of the essential properties of the effect of a causal complex.[32] That is to say: This effect is produced through all these causes only as a single one with a nature respectively differentiated, namely, as having the nature of cognition, as being restricted to grasping visibles, and as bearing the form of an object.

(b.12215 The contributory function of momentary causes)

(Question:) "What is the point of mutually contributing (*sahakāra*) in case of causes with unimpeded capacities, with immediate effects, and upon which as momentary a specific property cannot be imposed?"

(Response:) Contributory activity (*sahakriyā*) is certainly not in all cases the production of an additional property (*atiśaya*); it is rather the production of one and the same entity by many causes, such as by a final causal complex. Precisely this is the principal contributory character of contributing causes, because only this final complex is a cause, and because in this final phase, a specific property cannot be added, since there is no distinction for a single nature, because the arising of a specific property is characterized as the arising of a different nature. If, however, the generation of a different nature were possible, the complex would

[32] On the construction of *kṣaṇikatvāt*, cf. Yoshimizu 2003: 214.

not be final, and, therefore, would not directly be the cause. Thus, a specific property does not come about in a cause through contributing causes. These final causes, well capable by nature, arise together and, as momentary, exist neither earlier nor later nor separately, so that the effect is produced immediately. Among these final causes, the fact that contributing causes are contributing is nothing but the production of one and the same entity.

(b.122151 Causes come about as capable due to their causes.)

(Question:) "On account of what did the capable cause come about?" (Response:) On account of its own causes.

(b.1221511 A cause is not capable in the absence of other causes.)

(Question:) "Do these causes produce this capable one only in proximity to other causes? They might on occasion also be otherwise, and, thus, even a single one among them might somewhere produce it." (Response:) Even if these fabricated entities (*saṃskāra*) that belong to a continuum (*santanvant*) and have different capacities in each phase due to their relation with ever other causes, are identified as similar because of a certain similarity, their nature still is definitely different. Therefore only certain ones are the cause of certain effects.

(b.122151 Continuing: Capable is a complex of causes.)

Among these phases, the cause capable of producing a visual cognition is the complex of a visible, a sense and so on with a location unconcealed and so on. The specific cause as the ground for the mutual approximation and so on of these causes is capable of producing the actual cause of this effect. But these causes exist neither earlier, nor later, nor separately. Thus, the faults that would be given in case of earlier, later, or separate existence do not apply to these capable causes as well. For this reason, the cause of the mutual approximation and so on between these causes is the cause of the capable one. Consequently, the latter does not sometimes change. On this rule, the restriction of the relationship between cause and effect must in all cases be understood when the capacities of entities concur in each phase with ever other different natures, but not when the entities are of a lasting and uniform nature. For, since a nature does not change, it is not suitable that something with a capable nature is inactive and something without a capable nature is active.

(b.1221512 Refutation of the position that something is capable but produces together with other causes, not alone)

(Objection:) "Something produces together with others, not alone." (Response:) Is, then, the nature of an entity alone incapable of producing its effect? (Opponent:) It is capable. (Response:) Why does it not produce? How is it capable when it does not produce? (Opponent:) "Weavers and the like, though capable of producing a cloth and so on, do not always work." (Response:) The playful beloved of the gods who has been brought up in comfort, asks for work done to be done again! To wit: This point has already been rolled about with regard to the suggestion "as in the case of seed and so on" (cf. HB b.122). Since there is, therefore, no change in the nature of this capable cause, the fact that what has this property is of this kind cannot be denied, as in the final state of a complex.

(b.122152 Refutation of theorems regarding the occurrence of capability in non-momentary causes)

(b.1221521 Introductory alternative: If a capable entity differs from an earlier incapable one, something new arises; if it does not differ, nothing arises.)

If in the final state capability arises for something incapable earlier, this would be nothing but the arising of something new, if capability were the nature of this earlier incapable entity. If it were not its nature, it would not be effective at all, because the effect would arise on account of another entity counted as capability.

(b.1221522 Refutation of the position: a lasting entity is capable by nature.)

Moreover, does this non-momentary entity truly produce an effect only then, when all contributing causes are near? (Opponent:) It is seen as producing. Therefore we say "it produces." (Response:) Of great capacity is the observation of yours of mighty powers, since it assigns entities to various activities due to their mere nature, although they do not have this nature! This idea pains our mind, that when something at some time would somehow transgress your honour's path of vision, alas, it would as non-productive be deprived of continuation.

(Opponent:) We certainly do not hold the production of an effect for entities without that nature only on account of our observation. Rather these entities are effective for this certainly due to their nature. When we see them, we know that these are the effective ones. (Response:) True! Yet also the following is the case: The nature of these entities has the property of producing an effect. Therefore, entities with all contributing causes present do not lapse into indifference without having produced an effect. Has this nature with the property of acting without delay, therefore, come about for these entities only then, at the final state, or was it there earlier too? (Opponent:) It was there, because for entities with a nature that has neither been dislodged nor arisen, is stable and uniform, the absence of a certain nature at some time is incompatible. (Response:) Is then, now, someone a mother as well as barren? Or what is the meaning of this statement "A nature has the property of acting without delay, but does not act"?

(b.1221523 Refutation of the position: A lasting entity is not capable on its own, but in connection with other entities.)

(Opponent:) "An entity has this nature in company, not alone." (Response:) Then the one alone is one, the one in company another, because the difference of entities is characterized by a difference in natures. For, even in company, an entity is not an agent by way of another's nature. Yet its own nature was also earlier the same. Why should it, therefore, stop sometime to be active? (Opponent:) Also for whom an entity is momentary, why does it not produce for him alone as well? (Response:) It certainly produces, if it were alone. (Opponent:) Why is it not? (Response:) Because it is momentary. Regarding this point, it has already been explained (cf. HB 14,8-10) to what kind of entity activity belongs. How could this entity that exists for a single phase be otherwise? But what is otherwise, that is not the same (*sa eva*). Thus, this consequence does not pertain to our position of momentariness, because the natures of a producing and a non-producing entity, as well as their causes are not compatible.

(b.1221524 Refutation of the position: A lasting entity is capable, but its effect depends on the presence of other causes.)

Someone, moreover, thinks: "The nature of this entity has indeed the property of acting without delay. This nature does not depend on being accompanied. The effect, however, does depend on other causes. Thus, the effect arises only through causes accompanied, not through single ones." For this person, too, there is incompatibility under this position, for why is this entity actually also alone productive, yet the effect does not come about through it? (Opponent:) "It does not actually produce alone." (Response:) Why, in this case, does it have the nature of acting without delay? Has this point not just been thoroughly illuminated, that it actually produces? But why would this lasting entity which is capable also alone be indifferent to the effect while waiting for another cause? Disregarding another cause, it would rather produce that effect at once, because in this way it shows also its own capacity. By saying "the effect depends on another cause" you have stated that it does not arise through this cause alone; by saying "this entity is even alone of capable nature" you have stated that it arises through it. But how can these two options occur with regard to one and the same effect? Hence this person cries out distressed, with his vitals speared by the arrow of envy. So, he deserves to be ignored.

(b.122152 Conclusion: Contribution is only possible for momentary entities that do not occur separately.)

Being contributory defined as the production of one and the same entity is possible, therefore, only for momentary entities, not for non-momentary ones that can exist also separately. For, since their separate activity is possible, it is not appropriate that they have to be contributory.

(b.122153 The contributory function with regard to continua)

When, however, entities become causes by contributing to a continuum (*santāna*), for example, fire, water, earth and other matter, when boiled rice is produced from grains of rice or a sprout from a seed, in these cases the contribution of causes is explained as the production of a specific property (*viśeṣa*) by resorting to a conceptualized continuum, but not by resorting to a real entity (*dravya*) itself, because in a momentary entity a specific property does not come about. For, if by fire, water and so on an additional character of their nature is not gradually (*krameṇa*) produced for the grains of rice and so on, boiled rice and so on will not come about; nor will a cognition of objects come about, if for the visual sense of someone who has entered a dark room from a bright one an additional character has not been gradually produced in its continuum by its contributing causes.

For the senses and so on that are active without delay, on the other hand, there is no mutual production of specific properties. In this case, these causes, which have been generated through the respective conditions as the basis for their mutual approximation and so on as situated in appropriate locations and so on, become the cause of cognition with the accomplishment of their nature. Thus, among these senses and so on, the contributory character is nothing but the production of one and the same entity. Where, however, the contributing causes are conditions through their generating a specific property, in this case it is explained as the obtainment of another nature through these other conditions, because the continuum of the main cause depends on other conditions. When in this continuum of the main cause the earlier phases of the main cause and of the contributing conditions have ceased on account of their nature, a specific property of a phase arises, distinguished from precisely these earlier phases. Consequently, the effect comes about through the final bundle of causes which has been gradually provided with an additional character.

(b.1221531 Also in case of a continuum the contributory character consists in the production of one and the same effect by many causes. Explanation of the arising of specific properties)

(Opponent:[33]) "When an effect arises through contributing causes with an occurrent specific property, the arising of precisely that specific property (*viśeṣa*) might not be the case. If the specific property were to arise through something not specified, the arising of even the effect itself might take place. But then the contributing causes would produce the effect with no need to mutually generate specific properties. For this reason, even non-momentary entities with no need of contributing causes could be a cause. But an additional character of their nature would not arise through those causes which they are supposed to be in need of.

If also with regard to the arising of a specific property in the main cause likewise a specific property produced by the contributing causes were joining, in this way there would be an indefinite regress. Yet, the contributing causes are not always mutually in a state suitable for generating a specific property appropriate for producing the effect, so that the mutually generated specific property would definitely always be attached. For we see an effect's manifestation or failing when these contributing causes appear or disappear. Therefore, the first specific property would not come about for a cause without assistance from contributing causes."

---

33 The following passage can be associated with the strophes of TS 428-434 and Kamalaśīla's commentary (TSP 192,13-143,29), there attributed to a Bhadanta Yogasena, as well as in Nayabhadra's HBṬV f. 83b6 and 84a4 on HBṬ 130,21 and 131,8. This author would, then, have to be a contemporary of Dharmakīrti.

(Response:) We do not get tired of saying something again and again. If perhaps also in this way people might understand correctly, we will tell it once more. The contributory character of contributing causes is not only due to their producing a specific property, so that because lacking this capacity they would not be contributing to the arising of a specific property. It is rather also their producing one and the same entity (cf. HB 14,2f).

(Objection:) "Also this latter character might not be given for contributing causes that mutually lack a specific property. Or, if it were given, it might be given for them also separately, just as in the state of lacking this property. But in this way even the effect that comes about on account of this specific property might come about through a single contributing cause."

(Response:) All this has already been explained, namely: that in each phase a specific property arises in the continuum of an entity through ever other causes (cf. HB 10, 10f; 14,14f; 19,9-11); that causes which produce an effect are in specific states, such as occupying a suitable location (cf. HB 15,3f); also from what these causes arise (cf. HB 15,4f; 19,4-7); that, even if each of them is capable, they do not produce alone because the specific agents do not exist separately (cf. HB 15,5f); and that there are two types of effect, one which arises through a sequence of specific properties generated by contributing causes, such as a sprout, and the other, such as cognition through a sense that is active without delay (cf. HB 19,4-11), because the nature of the effect and the cause is different in these cases. When, among these two types, the effect comes about through a cause that depends on assistance by contributing causes to a continuum, the first specific property of the contributing causes does not arise through a specific property induced by contributing causes, like the immediately following effect. The specific properties following this first one arise through these due to the fact that this is their nature, namely, of this first one and of these later ones. Thus, there is no infinite regress. If in the same way also a non-momentary entity without an additional feature imposed upon it would generate an effect like the cause of the first specific property through contributory causes, let it generate! If this entity's nature is qualified as an agent without delay, since it can occur separately, it might be so even alone. That has already been explained (cf. HB 16,4-18,10 = b.1221522). Without this nature, however, even then it is certainly not productive.

(b.122 Conclusion: Non-momentary causes can have no contributory function.)

In the case of non-momentary causes, therefore, the contributory character is neither necessary for any in the manner of producing one and the same entity, nor in the manner of assisting to a continuum. Thus, there is no contributing cause for these non-momentary causes, and for this reason they would produce even alone. Mostly, however, we therefore see that the continuum of an entity situated amidst a collection of contributing causes produces its effect when a specific property has been imposed upon it by the contributing causes, such as in case of a seed. Thus, for one who proposes a lasting cause dependence on other causes evidently means the arising of another productive nature. One does not say, therefore, that something depends which does not have an effect, because it is not fitting that it does not produce when the productive nature is present earlier too.

(b.123 Summary of the arguments for the non-changeability of nature through external causes. Supplement: The melting of copper and other metals)

What has a certain nature, therefore, is like that through nothing but its own existence. But once having come to be, it does not again depend on the influence from something else for being like that (cf. HB 9,12f). An entity with the property of instability on account of its nature, therefore, does not profit from causes of cessation. Since also an entity with the property of stability cannot be changed by anything in its nature, what would be the use of causes of cessation? Or, if one admits a change, the entity would not be of just this stable nature. Thus, the first option remains, and with regard to this option the refutation has been stated (cf. HB § b.12). But that which is different on account of something else is another nature; and what is another, how will it belong to the former? For the difference of entities is characterized by the difference of natures. In this way, however, the former entity remains in its property of stability. Thus, it does not change.

Thereby the development of another intrinsic property such as liquidity in case of hard and so on copper and other metals through fire and so on is accounted for. Also in these cases, when the earlier form has vanished due to being annihilated on account of its nature, only another liquid nature has come about on account of fire and so on as well as of its material cause.

(b.1231 Refutation of the position: An entity is lasting and ceases through another. Cessation is not another nature, but the disappearance of the entity.)

(Objection:) "This entity has certainly itself the property of stability, because it abides when a cause of cessation does not occur. It ceases through something else, but what is called 'cessation' is not another nature. Cessation is nothing but the disappearance of the entity."

(Response:) This defence does not exceed the following two options: For him who with regard to the alternative "is the entity permanent by nature or impermanent?" says that it was permanent earlier and becomes impermanent later, there are two entities with different permanent or impermanent natures. For the first one assumed to be permanent he proclaims cessation and non-cessation in and of itself at all times. Therefore a cause of cessation is incapable in the earlier case.

(Objection:) It is not permanent earlier and, then, becomes impermanent later. Rather it is also later certainly permanent, because it is of one and the same nature.

(Response:) When this entity, then, because of its nature, does not attain cessation, why is it called "ceased," since its permanent nature and cessation are mutually exclusive?

(b.1 Conclusion of the establishment of the unsuitability of external causes of cessation)

If there is, therefore, a cessation of this entity, this entity certainly has to have the nature of cessation. Also in this way it has been explained that a cause of cessation is useless. Whether an entity, therefore, ceases or does not cease by its nature, there is no use for a cause of cessation.

(b.2 Summarizing the pervasion between the properties of existence (*sattva)* and of being a ceasing nature (*naśvarasvabhāvatva*))

Consequently, an entity independent in its cessation is necessarily bound to the state of this cessation. Therefore common presence and common absence are established in the form of "That which exists, is ceasing, and when the character of ceasing is absent, the character of existence is also absent."

(b.21 The general validity of this pervasion in the proof from existence (*sattvānumāna*))

(Objection:) "Although the character of cessation may be given on account of the intrinsic nature, certain entities might be also without this ceasing nature. For not every nature is the nature of everything. Thus, positive concomitance and negative concomitance are not established."

(Response:) This is not the case because it would follow that, if something were not momentary, it would not be real (*vastu*). For, capacity (*śakti*) is the characteristic of entities and the characteristic of non-entities is the lack of all capacity. But non-momentary entities have no capacity for anything because their causal function (*arthakriyā*) is incompatible with the modes of gradual or sudden production. Therefore, the pervasion "that which exists is nothing but momentary" is established.

(4.2 Effect (*kārya*) as reason)

(4.20 Definition of effect as reason)

If a factually different entity is to be indicated, the reason is an effect (*kārya*) because this does not deviate.

(4.21 This relationship is restricted to certain properties of the cause and of the effect.[34]

(Objection:) "If the reason is indicating through a relationship between cause and effect, then the relationship between the indicated and the indicating would be given in every respect, because the relationship between the product and the producing is given in every respect." (Response:) This is not the case, because something that comes about in the absence of another does not necessarily arise through that. Therefore, an effect is a reason for a cause with as many of its essential properties it is invariably concomitant because it is necessarily an effect of these. But the effect is a reason only with those of its properties that do not occur without those in the cause. (Objection:) "Then it would follow that cause and effect would be producing and product only in part." (Response:) This does not follow, because we think of the specific properties of the cause as indicated, when the specific properties of the effect produced by those of the cause are grasped, as well as of the universal properties of the effect as indicating when qualified by the specific properties of the logical mark. If, however, unspecified universal properties of the effect are meant, the relationship between the producing and the product is not accepted in every respect because these properties deviate.

(4.22 The pervasion between effect and cause is established through establishing the relationship between cause and effect.)

(Objection:) "Whence do we know that, even if something sometime comes about through something, everything of that kind comes about

[34] For the Dignāgean background of this paragraph, cf. Katsura forthcoming.

through something of that kind? But so, there is neither positive concomitance nor negative concomitance for an effect as reason."

(Response:) This is not a valid objection, because that which does not come about through something does not even once come about through that. For effect and cause are in mutual dependence characterized as being of produced and of producing nature. If smoke on this rule were to come about also through something else than the complex of fire and so on, it would not have a nature produced by that complex of fire and so on. Therefore smoke would not even once come about through this complex, like another entity. Neither would the complex of fire and so on produce this smoke, because it would not have the nature of producing it, like another complex. But it is also not appropriate that smoke has a nature produced by that complex as well as not by that complex, because smoke has only a unitary nature. Something that comes about through something with the nature of producing smoke and non-smoke would have the nature of smoke and non-smoke. This is because the natures of effects are caused by the natures of causes, or, should there be no dependence on causes, it would follow that the natures of effects were without causes. It is, therefore, the particular complex of fire and so on which produces smoke, and it is what is produced by this particular complex of fire and so on that is smoke. Because of the restriction of the natures of effects and causes in this manner there is no arising of an effect from a cause different in kind. Thus, an effect well-known does not deviate from its cause. Therefore, the pervasion of an effect with a cause is established when the relationship between effect and cause is established.

(4.221 Explanation of entities arising from some things different in kind, such as water lily-roots from cow dung)

(Objection:) "Do we not know of some effects that arise also from a cause different in kind? For example, the roots of water lilies and so on from cow dung and so on." (Response:) This is not a case of arising from some things different in kind. For only such a cause as cow dung is the material cause for starting such effects as water lily-roots (*śālūka*). Thus, the cause is not different. When water lilies, however, occur in natural continuity, they grow out of reed-grass. But the two that are produced from cow dung or the other have a different nature, although they do not differ in form. Since mere sameness in appearance is not a cause for things being of the same kind, because a difference in kind is observed in certain things even with the same appearance on account of a further specific character. For were this not so, if through a variant complex something non-variant would arise, there would be no difference and non-difference of effects on account of the difference and non-difference of causes. For this reason difference and non-difference of everything would be without a cause.

That is to say: When there is no difference because of a difference, there is also no non-difference because of a non-difference. But no nature of an entity whatsoever is beyond this alternative. Thus, for being without a cause entities would permanently exist or not exist since there were nothing to depend upon. For entities would be occasional through dependence, and there would be no regular employment of means for their ends. For, if the capacities of causes are respectively restricted, precisely a certain one would be employed in order to realize a certain result, not another one, because only the former would be capable of this task, and the other incapable, since these two differ in having the nature for producing one thing or something else. If the former were to arise also from a cause that is different from the one with a nature for producing it, there would be no respective restriction of the capacity for producing it. Then anything would be given on account of anything. In case, however, that the different causes' capacity for producing it were the same, the effect would be just this. Therefore, an effect well-known does not deviate from a cause.

(4.3 Non-perception (*anupalabdhi*) as reason)

(4.30 Definition of non-perception as reason)

The non-perception[35] of something perceptible as such[36] (*upalabdhilakṣaṇaprāpta*) is a reason for its absence or a reason for treating it as absent (*abhāvavyavahāra*).

(c. **Digression:** What is non-perception?)

(c.1 Dharmakīrti's position)

(c.11 Definition of non-perception)

(c.111 As property of the perceiver non-perception is, with implicative negation (*paryudāsa*), a perception other than the perception of the absent entity.)

When perception, in this definition of non-perception, is taken as a property of the perceiver, perception is an apprehension of his. Non-perception is a perception other than this perception of the negate, because it is other than the perception meant by this term, in the function of implicative negation (*paryudāsa*) as in case of the prohibitive attributes "not to be eaten" or "not to be touched" for a village-cock or a Caṇḍāla.

(c.112 As property of the perceived non-perception is, with implicative negation, the capacity for perception of an entity other than the absent entity.)

When perception is taken as a property of the perceived, perception is the nature of an object defined as the capacity to produce an apprehension with itself as object, because the nature of entities is capacity. Non-perception is, then, as above with implicative negation, a nature other than this capacity just as capable of producing perception.

---

35 For an explanation of the compound *anupalabdhi*, cf. Ogawa 2011.

36 For this translation, cf. Steinkellner 2013 II, 26-32.

(c.113 The determination of otherness in this context)

Under whatever circumstance the perception of an entity necessarily occurs when a spot on the ground is perceived, because their capacity for producing an apprehension is the same, that entity is mixed with that spot since they are mixed in one and the same perceptual apprehension. Of these two, when present, there is no apprehension restricted to the form of only one of them, for that is not possible. Therefore, the otherness (*anyatva*) of two entities with a nature of the same capacity mixed in one and the same apprehension is meant here[37], in the context of explaining non-perception, only as mutually related: That one of these two is, when isolated, in relation to the second the other than that. Non-perception characterized as property of the agent or of the object of apprehension respectively is the apprehension of that other or the nature of that other. This non-perception proves the absence or the treatment as absent of the counter-correlate (*pratiyogin*).

(c.2 In defence of this position)

(c.21 Non-perception is absence as presence of something other or of another perception with implicative negation, not with simple negation.)

(Question:) Why is the absence of something the presence of what is other, so that a treatment as absent is established by a non-perception in the form of the presence of what is other? (Response:) Regarding this question, we have already explained (cf. HB §§ c.111, c.112) that absence and non-perception are relatively given through the function of implicative negation. Non-perception is, in this context, not a simple negation (*pratiṣedhamātra*), for it would follow that a treatment of

[37] Considering how meticulously rational Dharmakīrti is when reasoning each of his points, this "here" (*iha*) strikes me as if he were resorting to a dogmatic solution of a kind I have never run across elsewhere in his works. It is not surprising that this solution has been critically discussed later by Utpaladeva (cf. Torella 2007).

something as absent cannot be established since a means of proving it is not established. Only the establishment of the presence of the one in unmixed form is the establishment of the other's absence. Thus, although it is the presence of what is other, it is spoken of as the absence of the one.

(c.22 The presence of what is other or of another perception does not prove the absence of something, but is the same.)

(Question:) "Whether the absence of the one characterized as presence of what is other, itself established through a valid cognition, would prove the treatment of something as absent, or the absence of the negate that is known through the establishment of that absence as the presence of what is other, there is no difference at all, whereby the establishment of the treatment as absent would be incompatible with the non-perception as absence that we accept. Why does not precisely this presence of what is other and the perception referring to this other prove the absence of the negate, but only the establishment of the presence of what is other the establishment of the absence of the negate?" (Response:) Because the absence of the one is not established as separate from the presence of what is other, and because there is no relation between the absence of the negate and the presence of what is other.

(c.221 The presence of what is other does not prove the absence of an entity,)

To begin with, the presence of what is other is not a means for proving the absence of an entity.

(c.2211 because the absence of something is not known as being different from the presence of what is other,)

What is not established when something is established, for this the latter is a logical mark (*liṅga*) or reason, as in case of smoke and fire. The absence of the negate, however, is already established with the establishment of the presence of what is other. Because the exclusion of the other is established through the same valid cognition which determines the state of that which is isolated with a nature unmixed in cognition with what is other than the negate.

(c.2212 and because there is no relation between the presence of what is other and the absence of something.)

Also, because there is no relation. That, indeed, is a logical mark for that with which it has some kind of relation. For example, the inherence in one and the same thing of the properties being produced and being impermanent, or of smoke the connection with one and the same thing, a hill, in case of what is marked by it (*svaliṅgin*), namely, fire, or the relation between the support and the supported, or the relation between the producing and the product. There is no relation whatsoever of this kind between presence and absence so that the presence of what is other could prove the absence of something.

(c.22121 The relation is not a relationship between object and subject (*viṣayaviṣayibhāva*) as between word and meaning.)

(Objection:) "The relation is a relationship between object and subject, such as between word and meaning." (Response:) That is not the case. Since a word is used when one intends to convey a meaning, between a word and its meaning there may be a relation of the word with its meaning characterized as the relationship between effect and cause or as invariable concomitance. But this scheme is not possible in the present case. On what grounds, then, would there be a relationship between object and subject? For, only if a relationship between a proving property and a consequent were established for these two, word and meaning, could there be a relationship between object and subject by virtue of this relationship. Yet precisely this relationship is not established when a relation does not exist; but if the latter is not established, there is no relationship between object and subject. Otherwise, if a further relation is not available, this would be a case of mutual dependence.

(c.221211 In a proof of the absence of something through the presence of the what is other, the consequent would not be a compound of property and property-bearer. The absent entity and the spot cannot be a compound when the spot on the ground is the other.)

Moreover, when the absence of something is established through the presence of what is other, the consequent would also not be a compound of property and property-bearer (as presupposed in HB 1,6). And in this way because of the statement "the absence of the pot follows from the presence of what is other than this pot" the pot would be absent everywhere at all times. (Objection:) "This does not follow because the absence is proved as it qualifies a property-bearer such as the spot." That means: "The absence is proved as the qualification of a property-bearer such as the spot, not as isolated. Therefore, it is not a proof of a non-compound as you insinuate. But there is a relation between the logical mark and what is marked because the presence of what is other is related to a property-bearer such as the spot." (Response:) There is no such relation, because the very spot and so on is what is other than this pot. For, precisely at which spot and so on something is said not to be present, only that spot is the other as unmixed with that pot. Through nothing but seeing this unmixed spot has someone the notion "a pot is not around." How could this presence of is other be a mark or what is marked by it?

(c.2212111 The relation is not possible on the basis of general and specific properties.)

It is also not possible to conceive in case of the presence of the other of a relation between general and specific properties so that the general would be the reason, the specific one the property-bearer. This is because, since the absence of the pot, as the general, is only known through the cognition of the specific spot, this specific spot does, then, not extend to anything else in kind. That the specific spot is not a logical mark, moreover, is due to the fact that it would be part of the content of the thesis (*pratijñā*). It is also not the case that the absence of a pot is established where there is a spot in general. (Opponent:) "It is precisely the absence of a pot at such an isolated spot, namely, one lacking a pot." (Response:) Is not the absence of a pot expressed by your saying "isolation of precisely this spot"? But this absence of a pot is established here already when the spot as the mark, according to you, is apprehended. What, then, is this a mark for? Also the search for a positive concomitance between the spot as isolated and the absence of a pot is in vain. Therefore, the presence of what is other is not a means for proving absence.

(c.22122 Also incompatibility (*virodha*) is not the relation.)

(Objection:) "There is incompatibility (*virodha*) as the relation. Because of this relation the absence of something is established through the presence of what is other." (Response:) What would be incompatible with what? (Opponent:) The counter-correlate (*pratiyogin*) of the absence, the pot, with the presence of what is other. (Response:) Do you perhaps wish to apprehend the counter-correlate, so that incompatibility would be the relation between the mark and what is marked? The absence of the counter-correlate, however, is not incompatible with the presence of what is other, because they occur together. If that absence of the counter-correlate which occurs together with the presence of what is other is to be apprehended, how would there be incompatibility between a mark and what is marked? Therefore it is clearly not the relation.

Also in this case the fact that the consequent would not be a compound of property and property-bearer remains as above (cf. HB 28,16-17).

(c.22123 The apprehension of the absence of something through apprehension of the presence of what is other is possible without a relation.)

(Objection:) Would not without a relation between the absence of something and the presence of what is other even through the apprehension of the presence of the other the apprehension of the absence of something not be the case? (Response:) We certainly do not hold the presence of the other to be indicative of the absence of something on account of some relation. Rather the absence of something is precisely the presence of what is other, as has been explained above (cf. HB § c.21). Already the determination of this isolated entity with a nature not mixed with the other settled in its unique self excludes in this nature the other. Thus, precisely the isolation (*kaivalya*) of that entity is the absence (*vaikalya*) of the other. Therefore, only the presence of what is other than that is the absence of that, and only the apprehension of what is other than that is explained as the non-apprehension of that. Otherwise, if what is other than that were not excluded through its determination, already a determination of the latter would not be the case, because entities of this or that nature would not be differentiated. Thus, definitely a treatment would not be in place on account of the observation of anything with the aim of acquiring or avoiding it somewhere. For, even when this person sees fire, he does not see only fire, so that he would not attend to this place when yearning for water.

(c.221231 Absence is not cognized through non-perception. Refutation of Kumārila's alternative to the position of HB 30,7f)

(Opponent:) "The absence of water is apprehended through non-perception (*anupalambha*)." (Response:) What is this so-called non-perception? If it is the absence of the perception of water, how would this absence be an apprehension of anything or the cause of an apprehension? Or how is even this absence of an apprehension of water apprehended? However, if this apprehension of the absence of water or an entity other than water is not apprehended by anyone at all, why is the absence of water not apprehended in states such as deep sleep, intoxication, swoon, the object's concealment, and oneself turned away? This has been examined in the *Pramāṇaviniścaya* (cf. PVin 2. 58,13-59,11). Thus, this person who yearns for water, though seeing fire, yet not determining that it is fire, not water, would neither linger nor advance. So, a quandary hard to overcome would have fallen to his lot.

(c.221232 Absence of the other is not known through the perception of an entity.)

(Objection:) "For that very reason the absence of the other is apprehended through the seeing of the one." (Response:) How would one know that the other is not present upon seeing the one? (Opponent:) "Through seeing precisely the one as isolated." (Response:) When we are explaining exactly the same (cf. HB § c.113), why does it appear to your honour as disagreeable? Therefore, although you have been roaming afar like a bird who does not find the shore, you have to come back again. Thus, enough of this proceeding in directions with no solid ground!

(c.221233 Defence of the theorem that the determination of the isolated entity excludes only that other entity which would be perceived if present)

(Objection:) If the exclusion of the other is already established merely through the determination of the other one, the absence of all other entities would be established equally at this spot, and not just of that one in a state equally fitting for being perceived. Also, the qualification that the non-perception of something perceptible as such proves its treatment as absent should not be taught, because entities that are not perceptible as such are also excluded at this spot.

(Response:) Contingent on the definition of otherness (cf. HB c.113), through the determination of the nature of the one the nature of what is other than this is excluded, because an appearance is apprehended that is restricted to the former's nature. For the nature of that entity is not the nature of the other. If the other's nature is, thus, not distinguished, the above consequence holds that one would be neither active nor inactive (cf. HB 30,17-31,2). Yet when cognition perceives this entity restricted in place, time and state in this restricted nature, it excludes that it is deprived of being so. For in this way that entity is determined by this cognition, if it is excluded that it may be otherwise; and the fact of its being so is given only for this entity, not for another. Cognition, therefore, indeed excludes things being one way from things being other. Thus, the function of a single valid cognition separates all entities into two groups, as being this and as being another, because this cognition is useful only in that it induces the knowledge of agreement (*anvaya*) and difference (*vyatireka*).

But that there is no further, third kind is already confirmed through establishing that all entities different from the apprehended one are pervaded by exclusion. For, if that third kind were not pervaded by being other than the one perceived, it would not be excluded from this entity by this cognition, and, thus, it would again follow that the entity has not been determined. Therefore, a valid cognition operating on any entity determines this entity, excludes another from this entity, and indicates the absence of a third kind. This is the function of a single valid cognition. That is to say: A valid cognition attending to any entity excludes only this entity from what is other than it, because it determines only this entity, and it excludes only the other than this entity from this because it does not determine the other than this in its place. Therefore, precisely this valid cognition indicates the absence of a further kind because, when this entity is being observed, it separates all entities as being other than this observed one, and it separates precisely what is not other than this as that observed one. Thereby also properties of a mutually excluding nature, such as gradual or sudden, have been explained (cf. HB 23,9-10).

Thus, in this manner through the apprehension of the isolated entity follows the exclusion of what is of a nature other than this, but not the exclusion of all other entities in its place and time. Therefore, something could be given that is not of its nature as well as sharing its place and time, such as taste and colour. Thus, the establishment of the absence of something somewhere at some time would be given only on account of the non-perception as explained above (cf. HB 26,3-7).

(c.222 The perception of the other does not prove the absence of an entity, because there is no relation,)

Perception, moreover, which refers to the presence of the other, we accept, of course, as establishing the absence of the one, the negate, but just not by way of being a logical mark. This is because also in case of this perception, the absence of a relation is the same, when the absence of the negate is a consequent separate from the presence of the other.

(c.2221 since the absence of an entity is the case only together with the perception of the other.)

Moreover, because the absence of the negate is established only at the time of the occurrence of the assumed logical mark. For, one does not apprehend the absence of that negate after apprehending the presence of the other entity and then establishing the positive and negative concomitance between the apprehension of that presence of the other and the absence of the negate. Rather one apprehends the absence of the one already when apprehending what is other than that, because one ascertains that this exists and this does not exist, without interruption, immediately upon seeing that other. Also because an example is not established. But that is a mark for this, with which it has a positive concomitance. For it is impossible to demonstrate that where there is a perception of the presence of the other, there is the absence of the one, because there is no perception of this isolated entity also somewhere else. If the demonstration were given in general, the same perception of the presence of what is other than that would be establishing the consequent property, because even in the case of an example, no other valid cognition is available. Under such an infinite regress of examples, the absence of the one at stake would, thus, not be apprehended.

(c.23 Conclusion of the defence)

Therefore, the absence of something is not established through any logical mark whatsoever. This presence of the other which is established through a non-perception characterized as perception (cf. HB 26,3f,6f) would only prove the treatment of something as absent in case of the mental performance of dimwits. Enough, then, of further proliferation!

(4.31 There are three basic types of non-perception: of a cause, of a pervading property, and of an intrinsic nature.)

This non-perception is of the following three types: when the relationship between effect and cause is established, the non-perception of the cause whose absence is known; when the relationship between pervaded and pervading property is established, the non-perception of the pervading property whose absence is known; and the non-perception of an intrinsic nature. Among these three types, also in case of both cause and pervading property, already the establishment of the presence of the other (cf. HB 36,3f) is the establishment of a treatment of a nature as absent. This so established absence proves the absence or the treatment as absent for an effect and a pervaded property. In case of the non-perception of an intrinsic nature, however, only the treatment as absent is proved through non-perception as the logical mark.

(4.311 The first two non-perceptions cannot be used as reasons with regard to entities beyond the range of perception. Rejection of Īśvarasena's theorem of "mere non-seeing" (*adarśanamātra*).)

(Opponent:) If you, then, assume: "A cause and a pervading property, whose treatment as absent has been established through a non-perception that consists in the establishment of the presence of something another than these, are proving the absence of the other, namely, effect and pervaded property, and this non-perception proves the treatment as absent only when these two, cause and pervading property, are perceptible as such," how can these two non-perceptions be employed in case of entities beyond the range of perception (*parokṣa*)?

(Response:) These non-perceptions are definitely not employed as valid cognitions, because logical marks are not ascertained in the realm of entities beyond perception. These two non-perceptions would only be employed in order to demonstrate that, if a cause or a pervading property is absent whose relation with an effect or a pervaded property has been established, then also the other, effect or pervaded property, is necessarily ascertained as absent.

(4. Conclusion of the explanation of the three types of the logical reason)

Therefore, precisely this **property of the subject** has positive concomitance and negative concomitance. Thus, indicative is as **pervaded by a member of the same** the certainly triply characterized **only threefold reason** because it does not deviate from its consequent.

(d. **Supplement:** Critique of Īśvarasena's theorem of six characteristics for a logical reason)

Others say that a reason has six characteristics (*ṣallakṣaṇa*), namely, not only these three prescribed by Dignāga, but also the characteristics that its object has not been invalidated (*abādhitaviṣayatva*), that its singular is meant (*ekasaṅkhyavivakṣā*), and that it is known (*jñātatva*).

(d.1 Refutation of the fourth characteristic: that its object has not been invalidated)

(d.11 Invalidation and invariable concomitance are incompatible.)

Among these three additional characteristics, that its object has not been invalidated (*abādhitaviṣayatva*), to begin with, is not a separate characteristic, because invalidation (*bādhā*) and invariable concomitance (*avinābhāva*) are incompatible. For, invariable concomitance is the occurrence of the reason only when the consequent occurs. But how would this reason as characterized by that invariable concomitance with the consequent occur in a property-bearer, yet the property of the consequent not occur in it? For, while perception and inference, when engaged in invalidating the consequent property, are eliminating this property from that property-bearer, the reason that occurs precisely when this consequent occurs promotes this property in that same property-bearer. Thus, alas, extreme discomfort abides by these logical entities to be proved.

(d.111 Incompatibility cannot be avoided by referring to different property-bearers.)

(Opponent:) "The reason is in other instances invariably concomitant with the consequent, not only in the property-bearer to be proved." (Response:) Why, then, does this miserable fellow, the property-bearer, aspire to have a son, the consequent, after marrying a eunuch, an inapt reason? If one has indicated that reason which occurs in a property-bearer even when the consequent does not occur, why is it said that the property-bearer possesses the consequent? (Opponent:) "Precisely for this reason the term non-invalidation is used." That is to say: "Just because the reason might also be otherwise, precisely for this reason is it said that the property-bearer has this property which is not invalidated by both valid cognitions." (Response:) What, then, in this case is the reason's capacity, since the consequent is proved already through invalidation because the absence of the consequent is bound to the operation of the invalidating valid cognition? Thus, in case of non-invalidation the consequent is proved. A reason is, therefore, useless. It is useless even in case of an invalidation, because it lacks the capacity for proving. If the absence of the consequent is not bound to an invalidating valid cognition, there might be neither an invalidating valid cognition nor the possibility of the absence of the consequent. Then non-invalidation would not be capable of proving the consequent.

(d.112 Incompatibility cannot be avoided by explaining non-invalidation as non-cognition of invalidation.)

(Opponent:) Non-invalidation is, further, not an absence of invalidation; it is rather a non-perception of invalidation. But this non-perception might somewhere be the case for a person even if invalidation were possible. This, therefore, would be the domain for employing the reason. (Response:) Is the reason, then, perhaps afraid of invalidation's perception, not of invalidation itself, so that you assume it to be employed irrespective of the invalidation, when you do not perceive it? This reason, then, is to be employed when invalidation is not perceived, regardless of whether the invalidation actually exists or does not exist. To what purpose, then, is this reason employed? (Opponent:) In order to prove the consequent. (Response:) Would this reason on occasion prove the consequent even if an invalidation were given, so that one makes no effort to determine the absence of this invalidation and employs the reason? Even so, that its object is not invalidated is not a characteristic of the reason, since the reason would be capable also in case of invalidation. Yet, just as the reason is employed in case of its non-perception while admitting also the possible presence of an invalidation—since for someone in doubt it is not right to act without such admittance—, so is it employed also in case of the perception of an invalidation, because when an invalidation is admitted, there is no difference between its being perceived or not.

(d.1121 Refutation of the position that the reason is incapable when an invalidation occurs.)

(Opponent:) "In the case of an invalidation the reason is incapable." (Response:) If it were so, a reason of which the impossibility of invalidation has not been determined does not deserve to be employed, considering that not even an employed reason may be incapable.

(d.1122 Refutation of the position that the reason is capable when invalidation is not perceived.)

(Opponent:) "The reason is capable when invalidation is not perceived." (Response:) Does perception pervade invalidation whereby invalidation is failing when its perception is failing, so that the reason would not be incapable due to a possible invalidation? Even so, the reason is useless because the consequent is proved already by the non-perception of invalidation, since in case of its non-perception, invalidation is not possible. If invalidation were not failing although its perception is absent, the reason's incapability would be the same. So the reason is not employed. Therefore, a reason which occurs also in other ways than with the presence or absence of its consequent neither strengthens nor undermines anything in a property-bearer. Thus, the mention of that reason is not proper.

Therefore, there is no co-occurrence between invalidation and invariable concomitance. Hence non-invalidation is not another characteristic of a reason.

(d.12 Non-invalidation of a reason is impossible in the presence of invariable concomitance. Thus, faults of a thesis (*pratijñādoṣa*) are also impossible.)

That, namely, would be a further qualification to this invariable concomitance, or deserves to be employed as a further qualification, that even in the presence of which other qualifications would be otherwise, like the characteristics of being a property of the subject and of occurring in similar instances. This is not possible, however, for non-invalidation when an invariable concomitance is given. Therefore, an invalidation with regard to the object, the reason, is possible neither for a reason invariably concomitant with the consequent, nor for a contradictory reason invariably concomitant with the opposite of the consequent. Thus, an absence of this invalidation should not be taught separately as a characteristic of these two types of reason.

Therefore, when a reason is employed, faults of the thesis (*pratijñādoṣa*) are not possible. Since, moreover, a thesis is not employed alone, the faults of a thesis should not be taught at all.

(d.2 Refutation of the fifth characteristic: that the singular of the reason is meant)[38]

(d.21 This characteristic is already refuted by the refutation of the fourth.)

By the above refutation of the fourth characteristic also that the singular is meant (*ekasaṅkhyavivakṣā*) is refuted as characteristic. In what way? As single, because it occurs only in the presence of its consequent, a reason does not deviate from its consequent. With regard to just this property-bearer another reason than this single one, moreover, would be incompatible with this reason because it occurs precisely when a property is present which invalidates that consequent of the single reason. Therefore this is similar to the case of invalidation.

(d.22 Specific refutation of the fifth characteristic)

Further: Is that one assumed to be a reason for a correct apprehension or its opposite, for which a counter-reason (*pratihetu*) is factually impossible, or for which a counter-reason has not been indicated? But what follows from these alternatives?

38 This fifth characteristic (*ekasaṅkhyavivakṣā*) and the sixth (*jñātatva*) are already referred to in the discussion of PVin 3. 37,2-10. It is, therefore, evident that Īśvarasena must have developed his *ṣallakṣaṇa*-theorem already before the composition of PVin 3, and not, as in Steinkellner 2020:764f hypothetically assumed, only before the composition of the Hetubindu (cf. Iwata forthcoming, 199?-201? with notes 468–476).

(d.221 First alternative: if there is factually no counter-reason)

If a reason is one that has no possible counter-reason, then this fifth is not a characteristic because that a counter-reason is not possible cannot be ascertained. Or there is no reason at all. For, neither is a proving property of unascertained nature characterized as such a property, as when its being a property of the proof's subject is in doubt, nor is one with doubtful characteristics a reason. Thus, none would be a reason. For, in case of equal characteristics, the observed possibility of a counter-reason raises doubt also when a counter-reason has not been observed, because in both these cases the reasons are not different. Or if there were a difference, then precisely this difference would be the reason's characteristic. For, a reason of which a counter-thesis (*pratipakṣa*) through this difference is definitely excluded, brings the ascertainment of its consequent about. Thus, without that characteristic it would not be a reason. But so, that the singular is meant is useless as characteristic.

On account of this distinction also Dignāga's definition of the antinomic pseudo-reason (*viruddhāvyabhicārin*) would be futile, namely, "An antinomic pseudo-reason is the case when two reasons with their appropriate characteristics occur in contradiction with regard to one and the same property-bearer." (PSV on PS 3.23b)

But the nature of this distinction is not indicated by you, upon whose knowledge we might foresee the possibility or impossibility of a counter-reason. Therefore, that there is no distinction at all must be suspected in all cases. Also for a reason of which a counter-reason has been observed, no difference whatsoever from the other reason is observed before the counter-reason has been observed. Yet also for reasons with a possible counter-reason, this counter-reason is not always perceived, although we have seen someone with outstanding intelligence imagining such a counter-reason. Thus, the possibility and impossibility of a counter-reason are not certain. Therefore, since the reason would have an unascertained characteristic, none would be a reason.

(d.222 Second alternative: if a counter-reason has not been indicated)

If the reason is one for which a counter-reason has not been indicated, as when Dignāga says: "When, then, soundness is assumed as permanent, then this audibility would truly be a reason, if someone were not to indicate also a reason for impermanence such as being produced." (PSV on PS 3.24cd)

(d.2221 Rectification of the misplaced appeal to this statement by Dignāga)

Now that this particularly grievous calamity has come by which should be neither exposed nor suppressed, how could it be overcome? To begin with, this reason, audibility, moulds entities, sounds, into having the nature of its consequent's true state, permanence; then it links persons for whom this audibility is authoritative on good fortune and final beatitude; then again, when its capacity for proving has been withdrawn by a clever person through indicating another reason, these entities and these persons have been deprived of the accomplishment of these respective states, this reason, audibility, proceeds to a penance-grove like a king who has lost his kingdom. So, what shall we say about this?

(d.2222 The correctness of a reason does not depend on the imagination of a counter-reason)

If, however, to be a means of proof is induced by personal imagination, what then would in reality be a means of proof or none? But that reason which by its nature occurs with this consequent property, how could it be changed, since entities do not change their nature and do not have both mutually incompatible natures? How, further, is a reason that occurs without this consequent property still at another time a means of proof for anyone?

(d.23 Conclusion: There is no counter-reason in case of essential property or effect as reason)

Therefore, because essential property or effect that, with the characteristics prescribed, are by nature invariably concomitant with their consequent, a counter-reason with these same characteristics, namely as essential property or as effect, is impossible. That the singular is meant (*ekasaṅkhyavivakṣā*) is, thus, not a characteristic of a reason because what is to be excluded by it, a counter-reason, does not exist.

(d.3 Refutation of the sixth characteristic: that it is known [*jñātatva*])[39]

Cognition (*jñāna*), moreover, is not a property of the logical mark. How could it be a characteristic of the mark?

(d.31 Cognition does not satisfy the conditions of a reason's characteristic.)

When considering on account of what sort of a mark something can be apprehended, the nature of something non-deviating is stated to a sensible person. By recognizing that nature, this person distinguishes between what is a means of proof and what is not, and, then, is active because he trusts that this reason will deliver the desired object. In this case, that which is this reason's own nature is a characteristic, but not the nature of something else. For, if it were the characteristic of something else merely because it assists in the production of inferential knowledge, there would be an undesired consequence: Since in this way the cognitional object, the cognizing person and the like, too, would turn out to be characteristics of the mark, because also when these are absent there is no cognition of what is marked by it (*liṅgin*).

[39] Cf. above, note 38.

(d.311 Refutation of an objection against the use of the attribute "ascertained" (*niścita*) in the definition of a reason)

(Objection:) Then the term "ascertained" (*niścita* in PVin 2.9c' following PS 2.6ab) should not be used. (Response:) It should certainly be used, because this term has a different purpose.

(d.3111 The purpose of the attribute "ascertained" and the purpose of its insertion)

For those, namely, who accept a reason as indicative through observation in similar and non-observation in dissimilar instances, there is no proper reason at all, because it is experienced that a reason is not indicative, even when observation and non-observation occur. The term "ascertained", therefore, has the purpose of conveying the notion that a reason is indicative on account of actual presence in similar and absence in dissimilar instances. Thus, the characteristic that it is known is not a further characteristic of the reason, because a specific nature of the logical mark is not denoted thereby. For these two, presence and absence, must be apprehended through the operation of a valid cognition that establishes the state of this reason, because no other way is possible. The term "ascertained" is, therefore, used in the definition with the purpose of revealing these two, although even through the mere mention of presence and absence the operation of a valid cognition establishing them is hinted at. For, otherwise, already their being given would not be established, since a decision about the existence of a cognitional object is based on the existence of a cognition. Therefore we hold that in every case already the decision on existence entails a valid cognition that establishes it.

A valid cognition is hinted at also because the composition of a treatise is for the sake of other persons in the sense of "the triply characterized mark informs you of the inferential object." For, exactly because it is meant for other persons cognition is established, since we hold that for those who do not know this nature of the mark there is no activity on account of that mark. Nevertheless, some logicians stipulate precisely these two, presence and absence, through mere observing and non-observing. Thus, the term "ascertained" has the purpose of refuting these logicians because, even if presence and absence are given, the fact that positive concomitance and negative concomitance are given is still doubtful. Since both, presence and absence, are ascertained through a valid cognition, the fact that they are given depending on that valid cognition is established. In order to convey this notion, we used the term "ascertained."

(d.32 Cognition is implied in the second and third characteristic of a reason.)

Moreover, because through the mere mention of presence and absence the reference to a valid cognition which establishes these is established, also on this account cognition is not a characteristic separate from this triple characterization. This follows from its being understood already through this formulation of the triple characterization in the same way that the content of an application (*upanaya*) is understood on account of the reason's being a property of the subject (*pakṣadharmatva*).

(d.321 Refuting the consequence that positive concomitance and negative concomitance would also not be separate characteristics)

(Objection:) Then also positive concomitance and negative concomitance would not be separate as characteristics, because through the use of one, both are understood. (Response:) This is not so. Since the reason's presence in the similar and absence in the dissimilar hint at each other, we say that a single formulation conveys both, but not that one is the content of the second. (Question:) Are not presence only there and necessary absence in the absence of that mutually hinting at each other? (Response:) This formulation respectively hints by force at both, because also one of them as communicating a restriction is not without a hint at the second.

Nevertheless, presence and absence by themselves (*kevala*) do not hint at each other, yet as bearing a restriction they are not by themselves, because a restriction has both forms. Therefore by "presence only there" neither is only presence expressed, nor also by the other formulation only absence, so that presence or absence would hint at the second. Cognition is not of this kind, because it is not different from a reason's being triply characterized on account of what <u>other logicians</u> behold. It is, thus, not a further characteristic.

(d. Conclusion)

Therefore a reason does not have six characteristics.

(0.4 Colophon)

Thus, the essay named "A Splash of the Logical Reason" is concluded.

Personal Names

Īśvarasena 2, 12 (n.31), 42, 43, 47 (n.37)

Kamalaśīla 24 (n.33)

Kumārila 38

Dignāga 43, 48, 49

Nayabhadra 24 (n.33)

Bhadanta Yogasena 24 (n.33)